T0142766

The History of Clyffe House

Five Generations of Muskoka Hospitality

David B. Scott

Order this book online at www.trafford.com
or email orders@trafford.com

Most Trafford titles are also available at major online book retailers.

Print information available on the last page.

ISBN: 978-1-4269-5565-5 (sc)
ISBN: 978-1-4669-4638-5 (e)

Library of Congress Control Number: 2012911901

Trafford rev. 04/24/2018

www.trafford.com

North America & international
toll-free: 1 888 232 4444 (USA & Canada)
fax: 812 355 4082

The History of Clyffe House

The History of Clyffe House – Five Generations of Muskoka Hospitality is a unique story about the oldest resort in Muskoka run continuously by the same family. The story, as told by the current owner, David Scott, is a powerful testimony to the value of tradition, family, and friendship.

In 1869, David's great-grandparents, James and Fanny Jenner, newly married in Gloucester, England, crossed the Atlantic for Canada on the maiden voyage of the steamship Prussian. They carved a homestead out of the virgin Muskoka forest and raised seven children. Tourism to the area became a viable option when the railway arrived in 1885, and the couple established Clyffe House, one of the first hotels in Muskoka.

The captivating beauty of Muskoka and the warm resort atmosphere resonate through the memories shared by the author, and those contributed by former and current guests and staff. After reading the story about this 131 year-old resort, it's no wonder that many guests returned year after year, decade after decade, and even generation after generation.

Author, David Scott, is a retired high school teacher and the fourth generation of his family to own and operate Clyffe House. David took over the management of the hotel from his mother and aunt in 1975, eventually moving home in 1989 to teach at Huntsville High School for the remaining years of his teaching career. David enjoys the beauty of Muskoka with his wife Arlene, his four children and six grand-children. David has also co-authored These Memories I Leave to You, a history of the Mary Lake settlers, with his friend and neighbour, Ryan Kidd.

TABLE OF CONTENTS

INTRODUCTIONS

The introductions to this book are written by two people who first came to Port Sydney as tourists, fell in love with the natural beauty of Mary Lake and eventually decided to make Muskoka their home. They have each made significant contributions to the communities of Port Sydney and Huntsville. I am proud to have them as friends and grateful for their help and support in writing this book.

By Hugh Mackenzie

David Scott's latest book, *The History of Clyffe House*, is at once a deeply personal story and a compelling picture of Muskoka at its roots. It tells the story of five generations of the same family who dedicated much of their lives to the hospitality industry in Muskoka, often under difficult circumstances and in a manner that affected the lives of a large number of people in Canada and the United States, over many years.

Clyffe House is the oldest resort in Muskoka still operated by the same family. Its continued existence today is a testament to the fortitude of those who envisioned the opportunity, created a holiday atmosphere that helped to put Muskoka on the map, and over many decades, evolved with the changing nature of hospitality and tourism in the region.

The stories that are told by David Scott, the current operator of Clyffe House, paint a vivid picture of life in this corner of Muskoka, bridging three centuries. It provides fascinating snapshots of early pioneers in the Jenner family, the tenacity of those that followed and the fortitude of the most recent generations in recognizing the need for change and new technology in order to survive in a climate where traditional resorts are quickly disappearing.

The greatest gift that has been given to people associated with Clyffe House over the years, is a taste of hospitality that in many instances has transformed into a sense of family and generational friendships. As David Scott has said, "You absorb the lifestyle and it becomes a way of life."

I can attest to this as I am proud to be a small part of the "Clyffe House Crowd" even though I have not actually stayed there in the past 60 years! And yet Clyffe House has profoundly affected my life, as it has so many others, as reflected upon in this book. The adventures that I experienced there as a young boy, the enduring friendships that subsequently developed, the opportunity I had to develop skills and character and my lifelong love affair with Muskoka all had much of their genesis at Clyffe House. Much of my family and social life to this day, still surrounds the Clyffe House crowd, Mary Lake and Port Sydney. For this I am forever grateful to the Jenner/Scott family.

David Scott continues to dedicate much of his life to the survival of the resort industry in Muskoka. He has been vocal about the issues that challenge this remarkable way of vacationing and he has pushed for legislation that would create an even playing field for small resorts. He has carried on a fine tradition of hospitality and is looking forward to passing it on to the next generation of his family. His book is a reflection of dedication and courage and I am happy to commend it to you.

Hugh Mackenzie has been a full time resident of Muskoka since 1967. He is a former Chairman of the District of Muskoka and a former two-term Mayor of Huntsville.

By Ryan Kidd

The most enduring indicator of the quality of life of a community must be based on the strength of its families, its traditions and its institutions. Port Sydney is a fine community. The importance of the contributions of the Jenner family and the guests of Clyffe House who adopted our village and put down their roots here cannot be underestimated.

A book about Clyffe House is thus a book about Port Sydney. A book about the Jenners is a book about the traditions of Port Sydney. A book about Clyffe House is also a book about the families of Port Sydney.

One envies the great summers that the families enjoyed at this grand old lodge on Mary Lake. People have been drawn back year after year by the camaraderie and traditions that have been built up by the Jenner/Scott family. You can feel this in the descriptions that guests have so generously contributed to the book.

I know that you will find this reminiscence enthralling. Dave Scott draws you into the fascinating lives of his family and the great times the guests have experienced in their summers at Clyffe House.

Congratulations to Dave, the Jenner family, and to the guests of Clyffe House!

Ryan Kidd has served as President of the Port Sydney/Utterson Chamber of Commerce and President of the Mary Lake Association. He is the co-author of These Memories I Leave to You – The Story of the Mary Lake Settlers, Trafford, 2003, and author of The Newcomers, Mary Lake and Port Sydney, 1870-1940, Trafford, 2011.

FOREWORD

Clyffe House is the oldest Muskoka resort still run by the original family, and, in my opinion, it takes a special kind of family to pull that off. Despite the passing of decades, I see the same traits in each generation: a love of people, a love of the land, perhaps a bit of foolishness, and a lot of hard work. The grand old Muskoka resorts are a dying breed, but when it's in your blood as is the case with my family, it becomes an integral part of who you are and I'm proud to have continued the tradition.

Clyffe House has been in operation for more than 130 years, and over that period, many things have changed. The most significant changes occurred in the methods of communication and transportation. The traditional resorts of Muskoka were made possible after 1885 by the railway and the steamship. The automobile brought more guests north while simultaneously facilitating private cottage ownership after World Wars I and II. By the 1960s, international air travel created new opportunities and challenges, as did global acceptance of the internet in the 1990s. Throughout these changes, through four generations of our family, Clyffe House has survived, and it is poised to continue into a fifth generation.

The loyalty of the Clyffe House guests and the value of tradition are prominent themes throughout this book, as evidenced in the testimonials contributed by our guests. We are proud to have families return year after year, many for decades, and a few even for a century. The ongoing success of Clyffe House is largely due to the loyalty of these guests and their enthusiasm for the family traditions that Clyffe House continues to provide.

I would like to thank all the guests and staff I've met along the way – some of whom are now among my closest friends and others whom I consider family – for the lessons they taught me, and for the memories we share, many of which you will read about in this book. While no one can say exactly what will become of Clyffe House in the future, I am pleased to know that the history of Clyffe House, as captured by the stories and memories in this book, will live on.

If reading this book sparks any additional memories, I would invite you to please share them with me via email or social media. Please visit www.clyffehouse.com for contact information.

Best regards,

Dave

CHAPTER ONE: THE FIRST GENERATION

JAMES & FANNY, 1869 – 1905

JAMES JENNER (October 4, 1845 – March 29, 1919) AND

FANNY JENNER (January 16, 1848 – January 10, 1930)

The middle of the nineteenth century was a time of economic growth. The invention of the locomotive, the steamship and the telegraph, and the shift to city living and industrialization in Britain all combined to encourage emigration. In all history there had never been a mass movement of people to compare with the exodus from Europe between 1850 and 1914. More than 34 million people left Europe during that time, and a large portion of them came to Canada.

James Jenner, 1903

In 1868, my great-grandparents, James Jenner and Fanny Leech, were working as servants in Gloucester, England. That same year, the government of Great Britain drafted The Homestead Act, designed to encourage settlers from England to immigrate to central and north central Ontario. The economics of it were simple: Britain needed lumber and lots of it. Ships could bring loads of squared timber across to Britain, but it did not make sense to have those ships sail back empty. The answer was to encourage immigration to Canada. Besides filling ships for the return voyage to Canada, England was also seeking to increase the available labour pool to work in the logging industry. It was a perfect fit - the settlers would become property owners, responsible for clearing their own land, farming in the summer months and logging throughout the rest of the year, and Britain would get the timber it needed. With the promise of owning at least 200 acres of farmland, James and Fanny married (in Woolstone, England, near Gloucester) and set out for the new world. At the time, James was 23 years old and Fanny was just 21.

JAMES AND FANNY ARRIVE IN MUSKOKA, 1869

Fanny Jenner loved gardening c1905

On April 22, 1869, the newlyweds James and Fanny boarded the S.S. Prussian steamship, which left Liverpool on its maiden voyage and arrived two weeks later in Quebec City, Canada. James and Fanny then travelled by train via Toronto to Barrie. From that point onwards, the closer they got to their new home stake, the tougher the travelling became.

From Barrie, they boarded a steamer, which took them to the north end of Lake Couchiching, at Washago. The next challenge was a bumpy stagecoach over the terrible road from Washago to Gravenhurst at the south end of Lake Muskoka. From Gravenhurst to Bracebridge was a relatively easy steamship ride; however, the next leg, heading north on the south-running Muskoka River with its six waterfalls between Bracebridge and Port Sydney, made traveling with any possessions impossible. Since Fanny had insisted on bringing as much as possible with them, even carrying with her a large, cast iron pot, which she called a kettle[1], the pair was forced to travel via horse-drawn stagecoach on the rough corduroy roads from Bracebridge to Utterson.

[1] This fifty pound cast iron kettle is still on the Clyffe House property today.

The final leg of their journey was a stagecoach from Utterson to Port Sydney. Fortunately, John McAlpine, the first owner of the Port Sydney sawmill, was there to greet them and paddle them across the Muskoka River to their property.

As they approached their new Mary Lake home stake, young James and Fanny saw a pretty, sixteen acre valley in the center of their two hundred acre grant. It was quite different from the flat English farmland they were used to: the valley was covered with a heavy forest and huge white pines that would prove to make farming very difficult.

One of the first things James and Fanny did once they arrived in Muskoka was to build a log cabin. They were able to deal with John McAlpine by advancing him $80 to buy the first saw for his mill. In return, Jenner was to receive the first lumber cut, for a floor for his log cabin.[2] The majority of the new settlers arriving in Port Sydney spent their first winter in one-room log cabins with no insulation and an open fire for heat. In mid-winter, the cabin temperature would often drop below freezing.

In 1870, one year after arriving in Muskoka, James' crop consisted of ten bushels of rye wheat, 50 bushels of potatoes, and 150 bushels of turnips. He reported owning no livestock. The census of 1871 showed that within the first two years of living in Canada, James had improved at least ten acres. He would eventually acquire livestock and build a barn.[3]

Also in 1870, James and Fanny celebrated the birth of their first child, Frederick James. Their second child, Alfred Ernest, was born in 1872. Five more children followed soon after: Robert, born in 1874; Ida, born in 1875; Roland, born in 1880; Alice, born in 1881; and Charles, born in 1884.

Adjusting to their new life in Muskoka took some time. Some of the following stories were taken from the book, Pioneer Days in Muskoka, which included a collection of essays by the descendants of the original Mary Lake settlers. Ida (Jenner) Casselman, James and Fanny's fourth child, contributed to the collection.

During their first year in Port Sydney, James bought a dug-out canoe made from a large white pine log for ten dollars from Jerry Hanes in Utterson. On October 4, 1869, after spending the afternoon with their friends William and Emilie Thoms (who had also travelled to Canada on the S.S. Prussian steamship), James and Fanny left for home in the little log canoe. It suddenly began to snow, and not long after, James and Fanny found themselves completely lost on the lake in a heavy snowstorm. After having paddled for hours, they finally reached land, and to their dismay, realized they were right back where they started. The Thoms' welcomed them back in and the Jenners stayed the night.[4]

The settlers on Mary Lake were surrounded by wildlife: wild geese, deer, pigeons, flying squirrels, lynx, fox and bear. In her book, Casselman tells of one settler, who, upon hearing a lynx cry out in the night for the first time, thought it was a person yelling for help. He bravely took his shotgun and started through the dense woods seeking to help the distressed person. He was surprised when told the next day that he had been following a wild cat.[5] When yet another settler first heard the deep sound of a bullfrog, he sat up all night with his rifle ready to defend his family.[6]

Casselman also wrote that in the early days, a number of Indians camped around the lakes. A feeling of fright was experienced when one or more suddenly appeared at a settler's door. The children were brought to sudden obedience when told the Indians would get them if their conduct was otherwise than good.[7]

Aside from building the cabin, the Homestead Act laid out additional requirements that James and Fanny had to fulfill. They were simple requirements, but they were strictly enforced. To receive the deed to the 200

[2] According to James' daughter, Ida (Jenner) Casselman, as documented in the booklet, Pioneer Days in Muskoka, 1927
[3] Canadian Census 1871
[4] Pioneer Days in Muskoka, 1927
[5] Ibid
[6] Ibid
[7] Ibid

acres, they had to clear ten acres of their property within two years and build a home at least sixteen by twenty feet in size. Within five years of filing a location claim, James and Fanny had to have fifteen acres of land under cultivation. They met the requirements and received their deed duly signed by Queen Victoria's land agent.

After fifteen hard years of farming the rocky Muskoka terrain, James and Fanny started taking in houseguests to supplement their income and decided to call their guesthouse Clyffe House. At that time, people from the city were looking to get out into the country to enjoy the clean air. People came primarily from Toronto, and from some American cities such as Pittsburgh, to breathe the clean Muskoka air that was widely advertised as good for one's health.

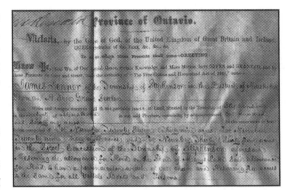

The original land deed issued to James Jenner

Any opportunity for tourism in Muskoka was limited to the areas that were accessible by steamship. A luxury resort had been built by William Pratt at the north end of Lake Rosseau, accessed by steamship from Gravenhurst. Alexander Cockburn built a fleet of steamships on Lake Muskoka. Unfortunately, tourism in Port Sydney was held back by the six waterfalls on the Muskoka River between Bracebridge and Mary Lake. Port Sydney finally had its first opportunity for tourism with the arrival of the train through Utterson in 1885.

While the journey north to Port Sydney was made much easier by the arrival of the train, the journey from the train to the guesthouse was still quite difficult. In 1886, Clyffe House guests had a choice: they could get off the train at Utterson and take a horse-drawn carriage or ox cart to Clyffe House, or they could take the train further north to Huntsville and transfer to a steamer such as Joe or Gem or Northern and travel south down the Muskoka River to the guesthouse. Many chose the latter route despite the additional distance and back-tracking since it was easier than bumping over the corduroy roads and through the mud or bad weather in a cart from Utterson.

By 1891, Port Sydney had become quite a commercial site. It was at the base of a chain of lakes and was so important that a lift lock had been built in the Muskoka River at the north end of Mary Lake to provide access by steamer to the three lakes surrounding Huntsville. By that time, Port Sydney already had a cheese factory, a grist mill, a shingle mill and a saw mill. The steamship Northern (built in Port Sydney in 1877) was used to carry these products to market.

The Jenner family and their guesthouse business continued to grow, so James and Fanny built a new, two-story farmhouse located in the spot that is now the front of the Main Lodge. The earliest photo of the building shows a typical, nineteenth century, two-story frame farmhouse with its dormers, steep roof-line, and large verandah.

The original guesthouse c1890

The farmhouse was then expanded. First, a one-story summer kitchen was added: an open shed designed to be a cooler place to cook on a woodstove in the summer heat. Then, in order to accommodate more guests, a two-story, six-bedroom section was built in place of the summer kitchen, which moved further towards the back of the expanding building. This progression of adding on sections to the back of the original farmhouse continued as their guesthouse business grew.

The expanded guesthouse c1900 (Robert Jenner standing center, Fanny standing far right)

The expanded guesthouse from a different angle, showing livestock sheds out back c1900

Sometime after 1891, James left his wife and family and traveled west. It is not known exactly why he left Muskoka, but perhaps it was the gold rush that enticed him. The newly opened railway to the west no doubt seemed to offer a golden path to a better life. The relatives out west said that James had left to get away from Fanny. The relatives in the east said that James had gone west for economic reasons. James never found gold and he never returned home to Fanny. Certainly, after James went west, Fanny, with seven children in tow, was left in a precarious situation.

In 1903, James signed a quit claim deed effectively turning over the Port Sydney property to his wife. The transfer included four lots in Stephenson Township, for a total of 202 acres. Fanny and two of her sons, Robert and Roland (the Jenner Brothers as they were known), began to expand the guesthouse and build a hotel.

Tennis on the front lawn c1900

Four of Fanny and James' remaining five children, Fred, Alfred, Charlie and Alice, followed their father west. Fred, the eldest, lived a remarkable life worthy of a separate book. His journey from Edmonton down the Mackenzie River and across the mountains to Alaska in 1898 was an incredible feat. I discussed his trip with him in 1963 when he returned to Clyffe House at age 93 (see appendix for details of Fred's remarkable life).

Alfred and Charles both died at age 28, Alfred of typhoid, Charles, a logger, from a falling tree. Alice became a nurse and a missionary.

Although Roland initially worked with his mother and his brother Robert in operating and expanding Clyffe House, he sold his interest to Robert in 1908 for $1,800 and followed his father and the rest of his siblings west.

Robert Jenner (front left) fishing while the Gem picks up guests at Clyffe House

James and Fanny's older daughter Ida remained in Port Sydney and married Lyle Casselman, captain of the steamer Gem which ran between Port Sydney and Huntsville. Ida's grandchildren still own property in Port Sydney adjacent to the Community Hall.

As part of his purchase plan in 1908, Robert built a spacious, two-story home for Fanny called the Homestead.[8] It had four bedrooms upstairs, a large kitchen with a cook stove and a living room with a large brick fireplace. The high, sloping roof was designed to shed the heavy winter snow and the wrap-around verandah provided an excellent view of the lake. There was a convenient walking trail running from the back of the Homestead to the barn that allowed Fanny to easily get to the cows for their morning milking each day.

Despite her lesser role in the daily operations of Clyffe House, Fanny managed to keep herself busy. She was passionate about gardening and planted beautiful flowers around the Homestead and the Main Lodge. She was also very active in the Anglican Church where she played the organ and taught Sunday school, and she was praised for helping other churches throughout Muskoka. When the new Port Sydney Community Hall was opened on July 1, 1925, she and Sydney Smith led the grand march in the opening ceremonies. She was very pleased that her son Robert was elected the first Reeve of Port Sydney that year.

Fanny died on January 10, 1930 and is buried at Christ Church, Port Sydney.

Meanwhile, James spent the last nineteen years of his life on the care-taking staff of the Brett Hospital in Banff, Alberta. He died there on March 29, 1919 at the age of 73. By that time, his family was widely dispersed across the West: his son Fred lived in Oso, Washington; Roland lived in Saskatoon, Saskatchewan; and Alice lived in Blackie, Alberta (refer to the Appendix for additional information on James' children). James' obituary states: "Among his intimates and co-workers he was liked and respected. The keynote of his character was honesty." He is buried in Banff, Alberta.

The first village council; Robert Jenner elected Reeve of Port Sydney, 1925 (from left: Hugh MacInnes, Mel Clarke, Robert Jenner, Bill Watson, Alec Hughes)

[8] At one time, Fanny lived in the house beside Wally Hall's cottage in Port Sydney; it was also called the Homestead.

CHAPTER TWO: THE GOLDEN YEARS

ROBERT & AGNES, 1905 - 1945

Robert Jenner deserves most of the credit for expanding Clyffe House during the golden years of tourism in the first half of the twentieth century. He first worked with his mother and brother to expand the hotel, building the Annex in 1905, but it wasn't until he purchased his brother's ownership in 1908 that Robert began a more ambitious building program. Robert added the Dance Hall and a new Boathouse with living quarters upstairs. He also built a two-story stucco barn, a maple sugar factory, two automobile garages, a laundry building, a concrete tennis court, large docks, and a large water tower. In addition, he cleared the trees for a ski hill immediately south of Muskoka Road 10 and he had plans to build a golf course using the area now occupied by Mary Lake Crescent. Eventually, Robert expanded the summer resort to host 80 guests on an assembled property of 400 acres with over 2,000 feet of Mary Lake shoreline.

The evolution of transportation was a major factor in the successful expansion of Clyffe House and in the development of the tourism industry in Muskoka in general. The train remained the primary means of travel until after World War II, which meant the challenge of making the necessary connections from the train to the hotel remained. Clyffe House guests continued to travel from the train by oxcart and horse carriage until after 1913, when automobile use became more prominent.

Robert and Agnes marry, 1907

In 1913, Arthur Clarke modified a truck to make a taxi to shuttle guests to Port Sydney from the train. As automobile traffic increased, so did demand for better roads; however, road improvement in Muskoka, especially around Port Sydney, was a very slow development. In 1915, tragedy struck when a car carrying Clyffe House guests slipped off the floating

Robert Jenner (right) brings guests back from church

bridge on Long's Lake in Utterson. The car, which was driven by the grandfather of Phil Clark from Utterson, broke through the wooden railing on the bridge during a rainstorm. The tragedy made the front page in the Toronto Globe. The accident prompted the Department of Transportation to close the floating bridge and blast a proper road through the rock on the south side.

Around 1920, in response to the increase in automobile traffic, Robert built a garage which would park about eight cars. While some guests drove cars to Clyffe House, it was still not the most common mode of transportation, especially since the early cars were not built for the hilly Muskoka landscape. The automobiles at that time used gravity feed for the gasoline, which meant they often had to back up the steep Muskoka hills.

Robert's expansion of Clyffe House is detailed in the following pages.

THE MAIN LODGE

Around 1900, the second summer kitchen was replaced with a proper kitchen. This new kitchen was a two-story addition similar to the previous six-bedroom expansion. The upstairs included four bedrooms for staff and the new kitchen downstairs was 1,100 square feet including the staff dining area and the pastry chef section.

By 1920, yet another section was added to the Main Lodge. This two-story addition contained a large, walk-in refrigerator on the main floor. The original ice house, which had been a separate building at the back, was torn down; instead, ice was now packed around the new concrete walk-in. The second floor

Stereoscopic photo of trees through Main Lodge veranda

had two bedrooms used for staff accommodations - one of which was large enough for four waitresses.

The dining room, 1928

For twenty years, Robert had been expanding the original farm house by continually adding new sections onto the back. By 1929, the time had come to rebuild the farm house itself. Robert redesigned the Main Lodge to include a large, forty-foot living room that could be used to bring the guests together for concerts, movies, or a quiet read by the beautiful Muskoka stone fireplace.

By 1930, Robert had expanded his original guest house to the 7,400 square foot two-story Main Lodge that could house eighteen guests and twelve staff. At that point, Clyffe House, which consisted of the Main Lodge, Annex, Boat House, Dance Hall, Homestead and other buildings including a barn and two garages (for guests travelling in their own automobiles) could accommodate up to 82 guests in 42 bedrooms.[9]

THE ANNEX

The three-story Annex was so named because it provided 22 guest rooms in addition to the Main Lodge accommodation beside it.

When the Annex first opened, there were no washrooms and no electricity. Each bedroom had a washstand with a washbasin above and a jerry pot below. Every

The Main Lodge, the Annex, the stucco barn and two tennis courts, 1920

morning, the staff would deposit a jug of hot water outside each bedroom door for washing and shaving and pick up the jerry pot to be emptied.

[9] There were even two small tent-cabins in 1931. The Jenner family lived in the three-bedroom White Cottage all year until 1925 when their brick house was built in the village.

By 1910, flush toilets had been installed at Clyffe House; however, there were only three installed in the three-story Annex – three toilets to serve 22 guest bedrooms! Of course, the jerry pots were still in use, but as time went by, it became increasingly difficult to motivate the staff (and the guests) to perform the duties required by the pots.

The Annex, 1905

Guests dressed up to perform skits on stage c1910 (Fanny Jenner seated second from left; Agnes Jenner's father standing with long beard)

THE DANCE HALL

Around 1908, Robert used some of the money from the sale of property to the north of Clyffe House, now known as Down Memory Lane, to build a dance hall. This two-story building was 1,000 square feet on each floor, and the ground floor had an additional 200 square-foot stage. To this stage, Robert invited bands, singers, magicians and choirs for the entertainment of his guests. Often the guests would dress up and put on their own skits. Robert often played the violin and Agnes played the piano for dances. Simple pine benches served as the seating.

The dance program shown in the picture to the right illustrates the formal nature of such events in 1922. Each night there were eighteen scheduled dances. The ladies had a dance program in miniature and signed up their partners for each dance. The dance styles were quite varied, and included the one-step, the waltz, the fox trot and the schottische. Strangely, the Paul Jones was scheduled fifteenth on the program – one would think that a dance designed to mix people up would have occurred earlier in the evening! Lancers and the quadrille offered something new in the second half. Of course, the last dance of the evening had to be something slow, and a waltz offered the chance to hold that someone special close.

Mid-way through the evening. after nine dances. the "sale of boxes" occurred. Normally each woman at a dance of that era would bake and pack a decorated box of goodies. which she would then share with her favourite partner during the mid-evening break. These boxes were prepared by the hotel and sold to the guests.

The Saturday night dances at Clyffe House were quite popular and local people as well as tourists attended. People would paddle over from Port Sydney. walk across the dam and "through the field"[10] from the village. or even drive down from Huntsville to attend the weekly event.

THE BOAT HOUSE

Robert built a new boathouse in 1908 that offered four guest rooms above and boat storage below. The rooms upstairs were lined with tongue and groove cedar as were the ceilings. and the floor was white pine. The style in those days was to put the hardwood on the ceiling and the softwood on the floor.

Downstairs. Robert maintained a small fleet of rowing boats and canoes. The rowboats were cedar lap strip with a pointed bow and stern. They had two sets of oarlocks to permit rowing from amidships or towards the stern. Of course. two people could row together if they were well synchronized. Foot braces were screwed to the floor for extra power. Brass screws held these boats together. Each rowboat had a tiller. which a person sitting in the stern could use to steer.

A dance program from 1922

One annual event which Clyffe House guests enjoyed watching was the launching of the swimming raft. Robert hired Jim Hughes who would use his team of horses to pull the heavy wooden raft off the shore and into the lake where it would be

View of Clyffe House from the waterfront

anchored out at diving depth. Jim used his team to launch the raft every year until 1960. Before 1908. the canoes would be launched directly into the water from a crude boat-shed on the north side of the dock. After 1908. boats were launched from the new Boat House. The Boat House had lockers built inside across the back and when people rented a rowboat or canoe. they were given a key to the locker with the appropriate oars or paddles. All the boats and paddles were numbered.

[10] The "field" is now the Mary Lake Crescent subdivision..

At that time, the Boat House also contained a row of change rooms at the back on the outside of the building. In those days, it was considered to be in poor taste to walk down to the beach in a bathing suit. Even in 1938, my father, Bruce Scott, was photographed wearing a one-piece, black bathing suit that covered his upper and lower body.

Even the dock has its own history. It originally went straight out into the lake with no breakwater. In fact, it went out so far that you could safely use a diving board at the end. The long dock was necessary for the steamships to safely pick up passengers. Today, however, there are by-laws against long docks on Mary Lake.

The new boat house with change rooms
along the back, 1910

FRANCIS (Nichol) WEILER (1904-2006) REMEMBERS

In 2005, I interviewed Francis Weiler when she was 99. It was a wonderful opportunity to speak to someone who had known my great-grandmother, Fanny Jenner, as well as my grandparents. Francis had a remarkable memory.

At first, Francis was hired by my grandfather to do kitchen work. She started by cleaning the kitchen and washing dishes, but Agnes quickly realized she was capable and motivated. Soon she was promoted to operating the separator. "Mr. Jenner used to rent cows for milk. He would milk the cows and I would make the cream and butter," recalled Francis. "The cows were kept in the fenced cow pasture up on the hill above the tennis court. He would gather the cows and bring them down for milking every morning."

A receipt for cow rental from Jim Hughes, 1920

In those days, renting a rowboat was the equivalent of renting a motor boat today and it was an important source of income for Clyffe House. Francis used to row across the lake every day to work at Clyffe House starting in 1919 at the age of fifteen. "Mr. Jenner loaned me a rowing boat, but I had to have it back early every morning and tie it up properly. He needed to rent it to the guests while I was at work. I remember that my family was annoyed when Mr. Jenner came to ask me to work for him. My parents didn't want me working at a resort where people were drinking."

Francis had a variety of jobs. She was also a housekeeper, responsible for cleaning the rooms and making the beds. It was her job to deliver hot water in a jug to each room for washing and shaving and to dump the jerry pots. She said there was a huge water tower providing water by gravity for the toilets, but "there were very few bathrooms". Since Clyffe House had no electricity in 1919, there were no hot water heaters. Light was provided by an open flame from carbide gas. There was a coffee tent set up behind the Annex and Francis also carried hot coffee to the guests' bedrooms.

The next year, at sixteen, Francis was again promoted, this time to working in the dining room. She still rowed over early every morning and made bread at 6 am every other day. "Mr. Jenner was up early too. He had to milk the cows and collect fresh eggs for breakfast." He was "crusty" she said, "but if you did your job properly, you were fine."

When Francis described the menus, I realized that the Clyffe House meals didn't change much between 1919 and 1960. Francis recalled the large vegetable gardens, and the cold root cellar near the tennis court that was used for storage. She remembered that my aunt Doris always loved to work in the flower gardens, no doubt taking after her mother, Agnes, and her grandmother, Fanny.

Francis recalled the change rooms attached to the back of the Boat House. "People were modest," she said. "Even the men wore bathing suits that covered their bodies. My swimsuit was homemade," she said. "I wore it under my skirt."

Francis told me that Fanny, who was 73 years old in 1921, would interfere with her daughter-in-law Agnes' instructions to the staff. Fanny was living in the Homestead at this time, Francis said, but she ate her meals at the lodge.

Two kinds of horsepower

"Mr. and Mrs. (Robert) Jenner would take the horse and buggy weekly to the bank in Huntsville. Mrs. Jenner was the business head. She knew her money backwards," said Francis.

Francis Weiler rowing to Rocky Island at age 98, 1998 (photo courtesy of Bev McMullen)

"I used to go in the regatta," she said. "I used to win the rowing race. I went to the dances in the pavilion at Clyffe House," said Francis. "They danced the quadrille. Mr. Jenner played the fiddle and there was a caller for the square dances."

In her no-nonsense style, Francis praised Robert. "Mr. Jenner worked very hard, and Mrs. Jenner used to get after him for working so hard," she said. "He was very interested in the Anglican church," said Francis. "We always got off early on Sunday so we could go to church at 6:30. He didn't go in the summer, but he encouraged the staff to attend; he did a lot for the church."

In a Muskoka Magazine article published in September 2004, Wendy Oke wrote a full account of this wonderful woman's life. On the day of the interview, Francis at age 98, jumped into our neighbour Paul Johnson's 1918 rowboat and quickly ferried Bev McMullen, the photographer for the magazine, out to Rocky Island and back. It was a very smooth, fast trip across the water. In 1919, Francis would have kept right on rowing past the island to her home on Mud Creek.

HOME COOKING AND PERSONAL SERVICE

Robert and Agnes' hospitality fostered extreme loyalty in their guests, and as a result, families returned to Clyffe House year after year, for decades, even for generations. Why did this happen? The Clyffe House experience is unique. It is difficult to pin-point any one factor that created such loyalty; it was likely a combination of the beauty of the location; the plentiful, home cooked meals; the relaxed camaraderie; and the welcoming and catering attitudes of the host and hostess. The reflections and memories contributed by current and former guests in later chapters certainly convey each of these aspects.

The home-cooked meals served at the resort were an important part of the Clyffe House experience. It operated under the American plan, which meant that three meals were included in the daily rate. Meals were served in the dining room; to help the guests stay on schedule, the staff rang the dinner bell one half hour before each scheduled meal; breakfast was at 8 am, lunch at 1 pm, and supper at 6 pm. If guests were slow coming up from the lake because the weather was especially nice, the dinner bell might have to be rung twice before everyone left the beach.

Agnes Jenner was in charge of the kitchen and their youngest daughter, Doris, was second in command. There wasn't the variety in the menu that you see nowadays – every week, the menu was virtually the same, and at each meal, everyone ate what was being served. The typical weekly menu was as follows (as found on an original hand-printed menu):

Mary Scott ringing the dinner bell

Monday	Meat pie
Tuesday	Ham with scalloped potatoes
Wednesday	Chicken with dumplings
Thursday	New Zealand spring lamb (replacing Muskoka Spring lamb after the war)
Friday	Fish
Saturday	Roast beef with Yorkshire pudding, choice of deserts, usually pie
Sunday	Turkey dinner with cranberry sauce

The Sunday meal was served at 1 pm, to allow travelers to start back to the city early in the afternoon and to free the staff to attend church. Cottagers and villagers often joined the guests for dinner on Saturday night or Sunday noon.

Having a farm was an advantage to Clyffe House, and Robert did what his mother had always done: grow the vegetables, collect the eggs, milk the cows, and use these products to make the food sold to the summer guests. When the cows couldn't produce enough milk for his guests, he rented cows from a neighbour, James Hughes, for $3.75 a week. There was no dairy service in Port Sydney, and resort owner, Bill Clarke, remembers that many of the local lodges rented cows.

Any additional food items (typically meat and fish) needed to be ordered, and the orders would be picked up at the Utterson train station and delivered to Clyffe House by Arthur Clarke in his taxi. Lake Huron whitefish and trout were shipped in from Whiarton by the Canadian National Railway.

THE COST OF RESORT SERVICES

In 1920, Clyffe House rates were average among the Muskoka resorts, about halfway between the very high cost of staying at Bigwin Inn and the lower range of rents charged by many of the resorts. Bigwin was the most expensive hotel in Muskoka at $5.50 per night and up; Clyffe House charged $3.00 to $3.50 per night. Deerhurst was listed at $3.00 per night and Grandview at $2.50 per night.[11]

A receipt book found in the Clyffe House office provided an interesting glimpse into pricing fifteen years later, during the 1935 tourist season. These records show that it cost between $14.50 and $18.00 dollars per week to stay at Clyffe House including three meals a day and a snack before bed. The record reveals that dinner was 50 cents.

[11] McTaggart, Bigwin Inn (1992), p15.

The receipt book also indicated the price of several other products and services, including:

- Transportation "in and out" from Utterson Station, as provided by Arthur Clarke in his taxi, cost $1.50 per person; transporting a trunk cost an extra 50 cents.

- Thatcher's Studio in Utterson made postcards of many scenes taken around Clyffe House and Port Sydney, including some aerial photos; a package of four cards cost ten cents. Postage stamps were eleven cents according to one entry on July 4, 1936.

- In those days, guests used the lake for bathing, but a hot bath could be purchased for 50 cents. The Main Lodge had one claw-foot tub made of iron that was extremely comfortable with a gently sloping back. As there were no electric hot water heaters, the staff carried hot water from the stove and filled the bathtub by hand before handing the key to the guest.

- A bottle of Orange Crush cost five cents.

- Laundering a dress was 25 cents.

- Car storage in the garage beside the barn cost $1.25 per week.

- A phone call to Huntsville cost twenty cents.

As an aside, I still have the old crank telephone from the office at Clyffe House. To ring the operator, you held a button on the side of the wooden box and turned the crank. The resort number was "4 ring 3", meaning, line four, pick up after three rings. To call a neighbour who was also on line four, you simply cranked out their number by hand. To listen to the local gossip, you quietly picked up the receiver.

THE VILLAGE HOUSE

In 1925, Robert and Agnes built a remarkable brick home in front of Christ Church in Port Sydney. It had several unique features: a beautiful Tiffany lamp in the dining room; a living room and a piano parlour, an early version of the modern family room; four bedrooms each with a walk-in closet; and a kitchen with a walk-in pantry and dumb waiter which brought firewood up from the basement with a rope and pulley.

There was a small barn near the village house, as it was called, to stable the horses used to travel back and forth to the resort. I remember being impressed by the images of horses Robert had painted on the walls of the stable. After 1925, Robert and Agnes returned every spring to live at the resort in the White Cottage. They moved back and forth, spring and fall, for the rest of their lives.

Agnes Jenner with her children c1950
(from left: Miza, Agnes, Wes, Doris, and Cay)

They continued to run the resort during World War II, but Agnes increasingly had to take over the responsibilities because Robert had become ill and was incapacitated. By this time, their youngest daughter Doris was running the kitchen and middle daughter, my mother, Catherine (Cay) had taken over the social and recreational aspects of the resort.

Robert died in 1949 and Agnes in 1952, leaving behind four children: Wesley, Miza, Catherine and Doris. Robert and Agnes are buried at Christ Church, where they both devoted a significant amount of time.[12]

[12] Robert helped build the Lych Gate and the Chapel at Christ Church. He built the original pulpit for the chapel and carved the dove on it. It now serves as the pulpit in the new church, as it was fortunately in storage at Clyffe House when the church burned down in 2001.

CHAPTER THREE: THE THIRD GENERATION

CAY & DORIS, 1952-1975

When Agnes died in 1952, she left behind four grown children, but did not leave behind a will. The four Jenner children were left to divide up their parents' estate.

Wesley inherited around 300 acres of property, and with the assistance of plumber-turned-realtor, Dan Bridge, he sold most of the property, including the property currently known as the Bridgedale and Mary Lake Crescent subdivisions. The eldest daughter, Miza, inherited the village house. Cay and Doris inherited the remaining Clyffe House property, at that point reduced to approximately sixteen commercially-zoned acres. Doris also inherited the ten acre Homestead, the thirteen acre lot on the north side of the resort, and fifty acres on the south side of Muskoka Road 10.

The Jenner children had grown up at Clyffe House, living there year-round until the completion of the village house in 1925. This chapter focuses on Cay and Doris as they took over the ownership and management of the resort. Wesley and Miza were never involved in the operation of Clyffe House, but there is a memorial to each of them included in the appendix to this book written by one of each of their children.

CATHERINE AGNES JENNER

June 12, 1913 - December 22, 2009

Catherine, or Cay, as she was known to most, was born in the front bedroom of the White Cottage on June 12, 1913. Her first cradle was a drawer from a dresser that was purchased from the Eaton's catalogue in 1907 and is still in the same bedroom today.

Growing up, Cay walked to school every day with her siblings – crossing the dam using the covered stairway built by her father that led down the rock face to access the dam walkway. At that time, the schoolhouse was located where Robin Hood Apartments is now, just east of the Muskoka River. Since Port Sydney had no high school, Wesley, Miza, and Catherine were sent to Mitchell, Ontario to attend secondary school. They lived there with Agnes' sister, Jenny Smith. From there, Wesley went on to study at the University of Toronto; Miza studied first at Havergal College in Toronto and then at North Bay Teacher's College; Cay went to Victoria University at the University of Toronto and later attended the Ontario College of Education.

Cay met her future husband, Bruce Scott, at Clyffe House while he was vacationing with his family. As the two were courting, Cay taught at Hughes Public School in North Bay. Cay and Bruce were married on September 14, 1940 at Christ Church in Port Sydney with the reception held at Clyffe House. When Cay and Bruce were first married, they lived in the west end of Toronto; Cay taught at Western Technical School in Toronto where she also coached the swimming team. Cay continued to run Clyffe House in the summer, heading north to Port Sydney with me in tow at the end of each school year (my father remained in the city to work and would join us up north on the weekends).

Cay Jenner (left) riding with guests c1930

18

Cay Jenner & Bruce Scott on their wedding day with Gertrude Scott (left) and Agnes Jenner (right)

In 1949, Cay and Bruce built a home beside the village house in Port Sydney. That same year, my sister Mary was born, on September 10 (the same birthday as my father). Cay began to supply teach at V. K. Greer Public School in Port Sydney. They worked especially hard to ensure that their two children received a good education. My parents sent my sister, Mary, to Bishop Strachan School in Toronto, and then to Laurier University. They sent me to Trinity College and then to the College of Education at the University of Toronto.

After the death of their parents, Cay and Doris became business partners and they continued to run the resort in much the same way their parents had for all those years. With excellent meals, personal service, and reasonable rates, most of the same families that their parents had hosted continued to return to the hotel each summer.

Cay looked after the entertainment, the dining room and the staff. Doris was responsible for ordering and preparing the food and also for planting and tending to the flower and vegetable gardens. My mother was extremely social and made friends very quickly and with ease, but she was also a strict employer – the waitresses all reported that they were very attentive when she gave instructions.

When it came to the evening entertainment, Cay was quite resourceful. If she learned in conversation that a guest was a painter, a photographer, a storyteller, a traveler, or a musician, she often successfully convinced him or her to participate in the evening entertainment at the Dance Hall or in the Main Lodge living room. She also held talent nights during which many of the guests would entertain each other. Arthur Beemer, an avid painter, would do poetry readings. He would recite "Casey at the Bat" and "The Hermit of Sharktooth Shoal"; he even wrote a second

Cay Jenner & Bruce Scott in their bathing suits on the dock in 1936

version of "Casey" in which the mighty slugger did not strike out. Meanwhile, his paintings were on display in the dining room for the month of August.

For several summers, Cay asked Marjorie Piggott, a brilliant Japanese-style painter whose family stayed at Clyffe House, to demonstrate her skills to the guests. Members of the community and cottagers around the lake were also invited to attend. With one stroke of her brush, Miss Piggott could paint a flower petal with several colours and perfectly graduated shades. She then sold the pieces she painted and donated the money from her demonstration pieces to Christ Church, Port Sydney.

My father, Bruce, did not play a significant role in managing the resort; Bruce had his own job as a salesman and later, as a policeman. He did enjoy the social life of the resort and often entertained the guests by playing the organ in the dining room. He also enjoyed golf and fishing.

Throughout her life, Cay was very active and enjoyed playing tennis and badminton, going horseback riding, waterskiing and she often entered the summer regattas. She joined in on the skeet shooting every Thanksgiving weekend, which was organized by Edward Barrington of Toronto, and she went hunting for partridge every fall with her 410 shotgun. She was an excellent shot and is often remembered for the time she left the tennis court mid-match to fetch her shotgun in order to take care of a troublesome squirrel. She took aim and fired, only to have two squirrels drop from the same tree.

Skeet shooting at Thanksgiving
(from left: Paul Whitehead, Cathy Scott, Rick,
Nancy Roberts, Cay Beemer, Gord Haig,
Greg Scott)

In 1973, Cay lost her husband to hemolytic anemia. Bruce fought the disease bravely for five years before passing away. He is now buried at Christ Church, Port Sydney.

Six years later, Cay remarried Andrew (Andy) Beemer, whose family had been guests ever since his grandfather, Dr. Nelson Beemer, had vacationed at Clyffe House before 1900. Andy's parents, Arthur and Mary, started vacationing at Clyffe House in 1910 when Andy was a baby, staying in the Annex. Andy and his first wife Cletice were friends of my parents' for 30 years. Shortly after both Andy and Cay lost their respective spouses, the two childhood friends decided to marry.

Cay was always an active member of Christ Church; she played the organ there for thirty years. The pump organ in the original Chapel would occasionally emit strange squawks because the church was not well heated in those days and the organ was partially frozen. Later, after oil heating was added, and an electric organ installed, Cay's music flowed more smoothly. She continued playing the church organ every winter until age 80.

Cay was also very athletic and she remained active into her nineties, playing badminton twice a week at the Port Sydney Community Hall. She also played bridge with the Merry Mary Lakers Seniors Club on Thursdays until age 92.

Cay outlived her three siblings and was blessed with six grandchildren and three great-grandchildren before her death in 2009.

DORIS RUTH JENNER
May 30, 1916 - February 21, 1989

Doris was born on May 24, 1916 in the same bedroom as her siblings in the White Cottage at Clyffe House. Born prematurely, she was so tiny that she was fed with an eyedropper for the first weeks of her life, and the midwife, Daisy Hughes, was quite concerned that she might not survive. In those first few weeks, as well as throughout the rest of her life, Doris proved herself to be strong-willed, and at times, quite stubborn. One such example occurred when Doris was in grade eight at the little red schoolhouse down the road. Her teacher criticized her as being a poor student in front of the class. Doris stomped out of school that day and never returned. Doris did not continue with school as her siblings did; rather, she devoted her time to working at Clyffe House and for Christ Church.

Doris worked at Clyffe House her entire life. She learned how to cook from her mother and how to garden from her grandmother and her father. In the early years, she carried on her father's methods of growing vegetables in the resort gardens and buying milk, fruit and eggs, locally. She bought strawberries from Mrs. Hugh MacInnes. Later, she began to order food from Canada Packers and General Grocers and she always had a large account at Watson's General Store in Port Sydney, but when Doris cooked a meal, it always included home-grown vegetables.

Doris Jenner a bridesmaid in
her sister Cay's wedding

Doris kept the Clyffe House guests happy and returning for years mainly by continuing to serve the same quality, three-course meals that her own parents had provided: there was never any scrimping. She would serve free snacks for the kids in the kitchen in the early evenings and for the adults as late as midnight. One guest in the 1960's brought his own weight scale and left it in the front hall of the hotel partly as a joke and partly as a compliment to Doris because no one ever went hungry at Clyffe House.

Doris was famous around town for her flower arrangements. When her friends' children were getting married, they frequently asked Doris to create the floral arrangements. Doris was one of the most generous people in the world. If she ran short of flowers because the wedding budget was tight, she would sometimes buy flowers herself to make up the bouquets. More often, she would go to a neighbour's garden and, sometimes without asking, "borrow" whatever flowers she needed to complete the arrangements.

Doris arranged the flowers for the many tables at the annual Cavalcade of Colour dinner in Port Sydney. She often had help from two second-generation Clyffe House guests, Helen Donovan and Ginny Haig. Together they would make the flower arrangements at Clyffe House and then transport them in a station wagon to the Community Hall on that first Saturday in October.

Doris also worked hard for Christ Church. She served for decades as the Altar Guild (a group of one) and as the Flower Guild. While she was known around town for "stealing" flowers for the church arrangements, she was a true Christian who never put herself first. Later in her life, when she had stopped driving a car, she walked across the lake in the winter to change the altar coverings each month and to place fresh flowers in the church each week. She, along with her sisters, followed the tradition set by her parents and grandparents, and was dedicated to the church.

Doris always took care of little details to please the guests: she provided fresh flowers on the dining room tables, and also in the guests' rooms when they checked in. When guests checked out, especially those who had been coming to the resort for a few years or more, she developed a bit of a tradition whereby she would present them with a bouquet of flowers to take back to the city. For special guests, Doris would dig up small bushes and plants for them to take home. For very special, long-time guests, Doris would occasionally send them home with pieces of furniture – such as a 1905 washstand, a wash basin, a water jug or a chamber pot. She was often generous to a fault.[13]

Despite being well-loved by the guests, Doris was very shy. Following her mother's and grandmother's examples, she seldom had her picture taken and she never took part in the social activities or entertainment organized by her sister. Her domains were the kitchen and the garden, from which she rarely strayed.

When combined, Doris' love of nature and her stubborn streak were a force to be reckoned with. As I entered my twenties and began to get more involved in the management of the resort, I clashed with Doris on many occasions. The main area of contention? I wanted to cut down trees that were threatening to cause significant damage to the structure of the buildings, but she refused to allow me. They were trees she had planted as a girl. Unfortunately, this attitude prevailed in many instances, and those instances compiled to create a significant issue: Cay and Doris were very focused on the food and entertainment, and while they were both excellent at what they did, they did not pay enough attention to the general repairs and maintenance that the resort required.

The fact that Clyffe House survived as long as it has is due in large part to Doris's stubborn determination to keep it going even if it meant she had to work all summer for a small salary. She kept the dining room open despite significant increases in the cost of labor and food, especially in the 1970's. The summer resort business was labor intensive – under the American Plan, the Clyffe House full-time staff included a cook, a pastry chef, four or five waitresses, a handyman and a handy boy. Doris and Cay were not carpenters, electricians, painters or plumbers, and so those tasks required the hiring of professionals. Meanwhile, increasing taxes and insurance, and the introduction of the minimum wage and unemployment insurance all became part of the economic equation, which was becoming increasingly dire.

---

[13] Or as I like to say, she was "Jenner-ous" to a fault.

In addition, the tourism industry was evolving yet again. After World War II, a significant number of tourists decided to buy their own cottages and the automobile made this decision feasible. Also, by the 1960's, air travel began to increase and Europe and the United States became popular tourist destinations. Both of these trends had a negative impact on the grand old resorts of Muskoka. In addition, the demands of the tourists who continued to travel to Muskoka were changing; they required additional amenities such as private bathrooms, which many of the old resorts didn't have.

By 1970, the stage was set for the closing of the dining room and the conversion of the hotel to a housekeeping operation. Based on the financial situation alone, the change should have happened in the 1950's. It was 1975 when I finally convinced Cay and Doris to close the dining room and convert to a housekeeping resort.

Cay and Doris continued to move over to Clyffe House every summer over the decade it took to complete the conversion; Cay stayed in the Ice Palace and Doris stayed in the Jenner. In the winter, Doris lived with her mother in the village house until 1952. Then she lived with her sister Cay next door for many years until around 1959. Her final winter home was in the lower Dance Hall which had been winterized for her by my sister Mary and her husband, Paul Whitehead. Doris died in Huntsville Hospital in 1989.

CHAPTER FOUR: FASCINATING LOYAL GUESTS

1900 - 1975

The tourists who became Clyffe House guests and who returned year after year were indeed a diverse group. They came from various countries including Canada, the United States, Britain, Japan, and Hungary, to name a few. They also came from every walk of life: they were architects, lawyers, painters, poets, engineers, actuaries, entrepreneurs, salesmen, professors - from every possible background. Yet, somehow, this diverse group of people was drawn together each and every summer. Whether it was the atmosphere of the resort, the skill of the hosts, the distance from their regular lives, the calming beauty of the landscape, or a combination of all of the above – whatever it was, it brought the Clyffe House guests together each summer like old friends. And it was likely this magical melding that led them to return year after year, even decade after decade, and in some cases for generations.

Despite their diverse backgrounds, Clyffe House guests have always had one thing in common: a love of nature and the outdoors. During the American Plan years, several guests demonstrated their appreciation by painting the Muskoka landscape, including Arthur Beemer, Wendell Lawson, Marjorie Piggott, and Freda Lawson. The rest simply enjoyed being outside and participating in the activities that nature provided such as boating, fishing, hunting, swimming, and hiking, sliding down the waterfall, and jumping off Rocky Island. Outdoor sports such as tennis, badminton, and horseshoes were also popular among the guests.

The Clyffe House guests were generally a very talented and self-directed group. While the evening entertainment was organized by my mother, Cay, it was often the guests who entertained each other. Some would decide to put on plays like Vivian Gundy and Hugh Mackenzie. Others would plan a musical evening, present a slide show, or sing at a campfire. Writers such as Wilson Macdonald and Robertson Davies would recite; magicians would mesmerize; and musicians such as Stuart Lawson or Norris Mackenzie would entertain. Tennis players such as Douglas Haig and Don Ivey were so good that people would take their coffee and dessert outside to watch the games after supper.

I realized later in life how lucky I had been to spend my summers immersed in this unique social environment. When the resort operated under the American Plan, the Jenner family was actively involved with the guests on a daily basis, and since so many guests returned year after year, they often became close family friends.

Loyalty is a theme that reverberates in the history of Clyffe House. We have always prided ourselves on achieving over 80 per cent repeat business thanks to the families who return to Clyffe House year after year - sometimes for ten, twenty, thirty, and in one case, 100 years.

This chapter contains letters written by people whose families vacationed at Clyffe House during the American Plan years, and provides a glimpse into the unique phenomenon that is the Clyffe House experience.

THE BEEMER FAMILY

The Beemer family history provides an excellent example of guests who have forged deep and lasting attachments to Clyffe House and to Muskoka. In this case, after two generations, the grandson of the earliest guest of the Beemer family and the granddaughter of the original owner (my mother) were married.

DR. NELSON HENRY BEEMER

Dr. Nelson Beemer began the longest family tradition of all at Clyffe House, starting around 1900. He was the first superintendent of the Mimico Health Center, a home for mental health patients located on Lake Ontario, west of Toronto. He was a strong believer in meaningful work as a form of rehabilitation therapy.

Prior to this period, such institutions were called insane asylums designed to control and safely segregate the mentally ill from the rest of society. However, Dr. Beemer was determined to create a pleasant, cottage environment on the shores of Lake Ontario for his patients. No doubt he was inspired in part by the peaceful resort atmosphere of Clyffe House.

ARTHUR and MARY (MUIRHEAD) BEEMER

Muirhead sisters on the beach (from left: Mary (Muirhead) Beemer, Winifred Muirhead, Louise (Muirhead) Walker, Arthur Beemer, Sidney (Muirhead) Haig, Ed Barrington)

Dr. Beemer's son, Arthur, and his wife, Mary (Muirhead), first vacationed at Clyffe House in 1910. By 1919, they had introduced other members of their family to the resort. Mary's three sisters, Miss Winifred Muirhead[14], Mrs. Louise (Muirhead) Walker, and Mrs. Sidney (Muirhead) Haig signed in at the same time with their children. Thus began a tradition that was to last three generations. Arthur and Mary Beemer had two children, Andrew (Andy) and Mary.

Arthur Beemer was a versatile man. At one time, he owned a company that manufactured Beemer pianos. He was a member of the Toronto Arts and Letters Club and knew members of the Group of Seven and was himself an excellent artist. He specialized in watercolour paintings of wild ducks and natural landscapes. One of his finest paintings is of Rocky Island, which is the island right in front of Clyffe House. It has been hanging over the Main Lodge fireplace for sixty years.

ANDY BEEMER (November 26, 1909 - July 20, 1990)

Arthur's son, Andy, came to Clyffe House as a baby in 1910. As a teenager, he went on canoe trips with my uncle Wesley. When Andy married, he and his wife, Cletice (Clarke), rented the Homestead until 1975. He started his working life in the mines in northern Ontario, but shortly thereafter, left mining to work in sales for a large Canadian aluminum company where he became Vice President. Late in life, he had a share in Extrudex, a Toronto aluminum extrusion business.

Andy and Cletice Beemer in 1917 Lakefield canoe

I spent quite a lot of time with Andy growing up, as his family was close friends with mine. Andy taught me the j-stroke in canoeing, and we raced in the regatta together one year. He also showed me his over-the-top slice tennis serve which I still use. He attempted to help me with my golf game, but to no avail.

As previously mentioned, my mother and Andy had been summer friends since childhood. Later in life, after they had both lost their spouses, they decided to marry. They were married at the United Church in Port Sydney on October 6, 1979 and held their reception at Clyffe House. Andy moved in to the house my father Bruce had built beside the village house in Port Sydney. Andy built an addition on to the home and filled it with paintings and antiques inherited from his father Arthur, including a Beemer player piano in perfect working order. Cay and Andy spent ten happy years together, entertaining frequently and travelling often to Europe and the Caribbean.

[14] Every Christmas, our family toasts Winnifred with "Aunt Winni's Cocktails": 6 oz rye; 3 oz whipping cream; 1.5 oz maple syrup; 1.5 oz lemon juice.

MARY (BEEMER) (1915 - 1989) and EDWARD BARRINGTON (1909 - 1985)

Mary (Beemer) Barrington and Doris Jenner in Clyffe House canoe #6 c1930 canoe

Arthur's daughter, Mary, became close friends with my aunt Doris. Growing up, the two often went on canoe trips together. Like many of the women who stayed at Clyffe House between the two great wars, Mary loved the outdoors and could paddle, portage, shoot, play tennis, swim, ride horses, and much more. Women of her generation were confident and adventurous and had given up the long dresses and clumsy bathing suits of previous generations.

Mary married Edward Barrington who owned J.W. Barrington & Son, a saddlery and leather goods business on Front Street in Toronto. They had four children: Joan, Jennifer, Michael and John. The family spent at least sixteen Thanksgivings at Clyffe House with the Haig, Donovan and Gundy families. Edward would entertain everyone at Thanksgiving with humorous poetry readings. He would also lead the charge in organizing the annual skeet shooting expedition. Mary always helped prepare the delicious Thanksgiving feast.

My first canoe trip was with their son John. We canoed from South Tea Lake down to Oxtongue Lake when we were around fourteen years old. We were foolishly trying to reach Oxtongue Lake before nightfall despite shallow water and frequent log jams and came within one hundred meters of plunging over Ragged Falls on that dark August night.

THE HAIG FAMILY

The Haig and Beemer families were the backbone of Clyffe House for over a century: the two families remained guests at the resort for four and three generations, respectively. The families were connected by two of the Muirhead sisters: Sidney married David C. Haig: Mary married Arthur Beemer.

The Haig family appears in the resort register first in 1920, and to this day, still spends Thanksgiving at Clyffe House.

Sidney and David C. Haig had three children: Gordon, Douglas (Doug) and Helen. The story of the Haig family is told by Doug's wife, Virginia (Ginny) (Gundy) Haig. Doug was a senior partner with Thorne Riddell, Chartered Accountants, in Toronto.

I asked Ginny to write about her memories of Clyffe House.

"My parents, Vivian (Clarke) and Bradley Gundy, lived in Montreal through the war and moved back to Toronto in 1946. Dad joined Time Canada in 1945 and became Vice President in 1963.

"We didn't have any place to summer and my Mom's sister, Cletice (Clarke) Beemer, suggested Clyffe House which she thought was wonderful. She had spent a lot of time there before she married Andy. We decided to try it for a week. "Cletie" and I slept on the third floor of the Annex. We instantly loved it! Then we learned that the Homestead was for rent. The next year we tried the "Olde Homesteade" for a month. After vacationing there for 18 years, we bought it in 1965 from Wesley Jenner.

"I do remember Agnes Jenner as a very gentle, kind lady. My husband, Doug, was very fond of Robert Jenner. As a child, he used to follow Rob around, helping him to repair things. Rob must have been very patient. He outfitted Doug with play tools and he let him help by the hour, something Doug never forgot.

"The kids all thought Dorie Jenner was very special and she was awfully good to them, as she was to all of us. Any time one of the kids got hurt, or stung, Dorie was able to make them all better. She had bluing to put on the bee stings and always an ice cream cone to put in their little mouths to stop the screaming.

"In the early days, I was in my teens and to me Clyffe House was wonderful. Friendly people, great food, and no dishes to wash! Just playing and swimming all day, a great feeling of freedom!

"My mother and Dorie became great pals. They took a practical nursing course together in Toronto one year. Afterwards, we always referred to Doris as "Nurse Jenner" and she got a real charge out of that. Mom enjoyed helping Doris in the garden and with her floral arrangements. They used to drive around and pick flowers in the neighbourhood, generally without permission.

"Doris used to do the flowers for the Community Hall on Cavalcade of Colour weekend, and when Helen Donovan and I arrived up for the weekend she would have the kitchen full of flowers that she had been given, or pilfered. She had to do arrangements for all the tables and generally wanted about twelve of them. She got both of us started and then would suddenly become really very tired and leave the job to us.

"She was the kindest, most generous, loving, infuriating person in the world. She loved the land and property and she did not like change. Cut trees down if you dare! She was a very bright lady and we loved her with all our hearts. I know that Mary Whitehead and Doris were very close. I'm sure that is what has given Mary such a love of and talent for gardening.

"In the old days, there used to be a laundry tent in the back and this is where they all did their laundry using the old scrub boards. When you consider the clothes they wore it must have been a huge job, long skirts, long sleeved blouses, and long pants for the men. The boys all used to wear long white flannels every Sunday. One Sunday there was a fire on one of the islands, and they all set out in canoes to help fight it. They must have been a real mess!

"They used to get dressed up in costumes on occasions, whether for a party or just for fun. Uncle Arthur Beemer did the makeup, painting all sorts of faces on them all. It certainly sounds like they were a jolly bunch.

"Tennis has always been a big part of life at Clyffe House and there were a lot of very good players, Andy Beemer, Gord and Doug Haig, Ron Maitland and many others. They all wore long white trousers to play. The cousins and their beaus, as time went by, would go out on the lake in the evenings in canoes. Someone would take a wind-up gramophone and records and they would join the boats together and just float along in the breeze.

"The spring below the front lawn was a great place to cool beer; Bruce Scott and Des Donovan kept their supplies there. Doug and I, in our courting days, built a wishing well at the spring with rocks we gathered from the river area. It was really quite authentic and Dorie loved it.

Christine Husband (left) and Debbie Donovan (right) ready for a roaring twenties skit

"My mom really enjoyed those concerts that she put on each summer. She was great with the children and it was amazing how much she got them participating. She and Cletice Beemer would sit around the fire every evening and write dialogue

Vivian Gundy's young actors ready to perform

and words to music for the show. Many of the Clyffe House guests would try to vacation during the time of the show.

"Our Thanksgiving reunions started originally when Doug Haig returned home at the end of the war. Granny (Sidney) Haig packed a picnic lunch and they all drove up to Clyffe House for the day. As was her way, Granny brought enough food for an army. So much so that they were asked to stay over and finish it up the next day. I think this was our first Thanksgiving at Clyffe House. What a party was launched!

"Granny Haig, thanks to Nellie, her maid, always brought enough food for three days and mighty good eating it was. Some of the real treats were the small patisserie cakes she brought—dozens of them—and they were readily available all weekend. On Saturday evening, Arthur Beemer would recite "Casey at the Bat" and Ed Barrington would read "The Hermit of Sharktooth Shoal" and these would always bring down the house. Cay would play the piano. "Bless This House" was her favourite. She always worried that the pipes would freeze and I am afraid they would quite often. Bruce's job was cooking the steaks for dinner and I think he would be frozen through, but I know he got a big kick out of it.

"Now, sixty years later, my family is still enjoying Thanksgiving at Clyffe House with the Beemers, Donovans and Jenners!"

Thanksgiving tradition at Clyffe House with the Scott/Haig/Donovan families - 70th year, 2015

Ginny and her husband Doug had two children, Bradley and Gordon. Gord lives year-round on Mary Lake in a house built on the Homestead property where Ginny visits in the summer.

Contributed by Ginny Haig (December 2005)

Ginny Haig with her family
(from left: Brad, Ginny, Doug and Gord)

HELEN (HAIG) (1924 – 1997) and DESMOND DONOVAN (1911 - 1955)

Helen Donovan, Clyffe House guest
for 72 years

Helen (Haig) Donovan vacationed at Clyffe House every July and August for her entire life.

She was the daughter of David and Sidney (Muirhead) Haig. Mr. Haig was a founder of Haig, Rennie & CO., stockbrokers. He was a member of the Toronto Stock Exchange and President of the Granite Club from 1939 to 1941.

Helen stayed in the Annex for 72 consecutive summers. She took her meals with her mother Sidney and her aunts, Winifred Muirhead and Mary Beemer, at the long table at the head of the dining room reserved for the whole summer for her extended family.

Helen married Desmond Donovan and they had three children: Deborah, Douglas, and Peter. Helen also had a stepdaughter, Patsy, and a stepson, Murray.

Helen was an excellent tennis player. For many years, she entertained the Clyffe House guests after supper, playing mixed doubles with her brother, Doug, her cousin, Andy Beemer, and fellow guests, Stuart Lawson, Jack Bond, Ron Maitland, Don Ivey and many others. She played ladies' doubles with her sister-in-law, Ginny Haig, and her friend Cay Scott, among others. She had the smoothest, most accurate forehand cross-court shots of any of the Clyffe House players.

When the dining room closed in 1975, the bedrooms that Helen and her parents had rented since 1920 on the ground floor of the Annex were converted into a housekeeping cottage, which Helen rented from June until September every year from 1975 to 1997.

With the dining room closed, Cay had much more time to spend with her friend Helen. The two would go swimming every morning, and then have their sherry behind the Annex, followed by their lunch. After lunch, it was off to the beach for another swim, followed by an afternoon nap in the sun at the beach beside the Boat House, another swim and then back up to the cottage for cocktails and dinner.

Helen's three children each married and brought their own children up to Clyffe House allowing Helen to spend the summers with her seven grandchildren. Debbie married Hugh Harbinson and they have two children, Kelly and Andrew; Doug married Margaret and they have two sons, Jeffrey and Michael. Peter passed away in 2014 after a brave battle with cancer leaving behind two daughters, Christine and Jennifer, and one step-daughter, Laurie. Peter and his partner, Dena Maule, continued to bring their children and grandchildren to Clyffe House each year to continue the tradition.

Helen's family still spends Thanksgiving weekend at Clyffe House with my family and my sister's family, along with Ginny Haig, her son Gord and other family and friends. The younger generation has become quite close-knit: Helen's granddaughter Kelly was a bridesmaid in my sister Mary's daughter Jenna's wedding party and her grandson Andrew was a groomsman in Mary's son Scott's wedding party.

Debbie (Donovan) Harbinson now owns her own Mary Lake cottage in the same bay as Clyffe House, and her brother Doug now owns a cottage next door to the Homestead.

THE LOVATT FAMILY: GEORGE, LILY, GARRY and JACK

George and Lily Lovatt first came to Clyffe House in the 1920s. The summer they met, George was a guest at Clyffe House, and Lily, who was staying at a neighboring cottage, was visiting the hotel. She first saw George playing in a baseball game on the front lawn at Clyffe House. They met, but nothing developed. Some years later, they re-connected in Toronto. They married in 1926 and vacationed at Clyffe House until the war.

George, who had graduated from law school in 1926, owned a 1928 Studebaker automobile; however, due to gasoline rationing during the war, the Lovatts took the train to Utterson. Mabel Paterson (once a chauffeur to Winston Churchill) then brought them to Clyffe House in her taxi.

I interviewed their son, Garry, in the fall of 2006.

Garry was only ten in 1948, but he remembers that Clyffe House guests dressed formally for dinner, especially Sunday noon dinner. "Debbie Donovan had an endless set of sun-suits with ruffles," he recalled. He remembered that his mother and Doris Jenner both loved flowers and flower arranging. "Doris had flowers on the dresser in the bedroom when we arrived and there were always arrangements on the dining room tables."

Horseshoes on the front lawn
(from left: George Lovatt, George Hutchings, Don Ivey and Chris Husband)

"Parents didn't have to worry about their kids' safety at Clyffe House. We had tremendous freedom," Garry said. He remembered many guests, including Ralph Raymer, Christine Matson and her brother Raymor Matson from New York. Garry admitted to being jealous of Raymor and Tony Lawson because they each had fast motorboats.

Garry remembered many hours of peace and tranquility while paddling a cedar strip canoe on Mary Lake. "I often think of how the lake changed over the years. The first year I was there, in 1948, Dad often took Mom and me for a row after dinner. It was always so quiet and still in the evenings. I heard my first loon that summer. Very few people had outboards then. Although noisy, they were too slow for water skiing or just buzzing around and so they didn't get much use. By Sunday evening everything returned to being still and quiet. Within two or three years, much bigger, more powerful outboards had become common."

He recalled James Houston who had spent a year at Cape Dorset and had bought Eskimo carvings to display. He spoke of Walter Rennie who wrote a grammar textbook in the upper Dance Hall. Garry also remembered architect Wendell Lawson and his wife Isobel: Wendell designed my parents' house in Port Sydney.

Garry loved the Japanese style watercolour paintings of Marjorie Piggott. Marjorie and her sister, Edith, used to send Garry out to collect birch bark on which Marjorie would paint delicate flowers.

Other guests recalled were Reverend David Andrews, a professor at Knox College, Toronto and his wife and two children, David and Catherine. Many guests came from the Lawrence Park area and quite a few belonged to the Toronto Lawn Tennis Club.

Garry's brother Jack Lovatt and his wife Valerie also vacationed at Clyffe House with their children. In 2008, they returned to Clyffe House to celebrate Jack's 80th birthday.

Guests standing on the terrace in 1958 (Cay and Mary Scott on the left; Garry Lovatt second from right; George Lovatt fifth from right)

THE POWER FAMILY: BRUCE, CHARLOTTE, ELIZABETH and MARY

Charlotte and Bruce Power began vacationing at Clyffe House in the 1940s. I remember Bruce as being a very serious man and no wonder - he was Chief Actuary for the Canadian Life Insurance Officers Association in Toronto. I remember Charlotte Power for her beautiful and warm smile. I asked their daughter Elizabeth to record her memories for this book.

"We always came for three weeks in August. Dad, Mom, Mary and I stayed in a room at the top of the stairs on the second floor of the Annex. When I think of it now, I don't know how my Mom managed. I don't remember any closets in the room and of course four of us were all sharing the same space.

"In many of the photos we children were dressed in pretty little smocked dresses, not shorts, and of course the clothes all had to be hung out to dry after they were washed. Oh, how times have changed! Mom probably ironed them too. I remember the Annex so well with only one bathroom on each floor and everyone taking turns getting ready for breakfast in the morning. I also remember the washbasin and jug in each room. I went down to the spring with my Dad to get the water each day. We used it to wash our faces and hands in the morning while waiting for the bathroom and boy was the water ever cold on late summer mornings!

"We walked regularly to Port Sydney, past the homestead, through the fields and over the dam. As young children, one of our favorite pastimes en route to the dam was finding as many "touch-me-nots" as we could and squeezing the pods to make the seeds spring out. We usually got a treat in town and always stopped at the dam on the way. I recall one occasion in the early years when Judy Raymer stepped in a "cow pie" on our way through the field.

Guests show off their sundresses (from left: Libby Power, Sue Ogilvie, Mary Power, Frances Burrell)

"I remember as a very young child spending many hours out on the front lawn trying to catch grasshoppers in a glass jar for the fishermen. When I was old enough my dad took me out fishing with him. Dorie used to cook the fish we caught if we asked her to.

"I think one of the things that attracted everyone to Clyffe House was how at home and welcome we all felt there, both adults and children alike. The same guests seemed to return year after year and we always looked forward to spending our holiday in the company of good friends.

"The meals were outstanding and something both the old and young looked forward to. There are times even now when I'll smell some wonderful aroma and it will take me back to Clyffe House."

Contributed by Elizabeth Power (January 2007)

THE LAWSON FAMILY: STUART, FREDA, TONY and CHRISTOPHER

Between 1946 and 1966, the Lawson family made a huge contribution to Clyffe House. Stuart and Freda and their two sons, Tony and Christopher, spent twenty years in the Boat House. Now Tony has his own beautiful cottage on Mary Lake.

In February 2006, I asked Tony to recall the early days.

"My parents first came to Muskoka in 1910. Dad was orchestra leader at Cleveland's House for three years and played the violin. He was once offered land instead of money for working there. He didn't take the land.

"In 1946, my parents visited Clyffe House to have lunch with my Uncle Wendell and Aunt Isobel Lawson, who were spending their honeymoon there. Wendell met his wife to be, Isobel Garbutt, at Trinity Anglican

Stuart and Freda Lawson on the Boathouse veranda; in their Yacht Club party costumes; Freda reading to the children

Church in 1945. They had heard of Clyffe House because Isobel was raised by the Sisters of St. John the Divine. who have their summer retreat in Port Sydney.

"My parents wanted to come back to Clyffe House as a family. which we did that year. We stayed in the Annex on the ground floor in the front two rooms for two weeks.

"We came up for about two to four weeks in the early years. but in 1949 we were able to rent the Boat House for the whole season of nine weeks. There was an outhouse and no plumbing. and four bedrooms. Around 1950. my Dad and I took out a wall so that we had two bedrooms and a combination living/dining area. Then we got indoor plumbing. but we still used an ice box. with ice delivered twice a week. I remember cleaning the sawdust off the ice blocks. As the ice melted. it was supposed to drip into a pan. but we would forget to empty it. The solution was to drill a hole in the wooden floor under the icebox and let the water drip through to the boathouse below.

"One summer. a couple arrived on their honeymoon. and we found out the man was an Ontario horseshoe champion. Dad organized a crew to build a regulation horseshoe pit. This champion then taught us how to pitch horseshoes. I will always remember the one and a half turns he taught us. He could throw 40 ringers in a row.

"I took everybody waterskiing on the weekend when five gallons of gas cost $2.50. We would ski from 2:30 pm to 5:30 pm. I taught over 500 people over a twenty year span. including Hughie Mackenzie. We were even filmed by a CFTO TV crew on the safety of water skiing. We broke every rule in the book to produce this film with Harvey Kirk. and producer/director John Spalding. They had a camera man and a script assistant with them. and spent the whole day at Clyffe House. I taught Doug Donovan to ski on this show. "

What Tony was reluctant to recall, speaking of safety, was that he almost died on the shoot. At one point, Tony was demonstrating slalom skiing technique, but he failed to notice that his father had driven the boat too close to the main dock. Helen Donovan remembered sitting on the dock in shock while Tony literally flew over the fourteen foot wide structure and fell in the water on the other side. Unfortunately, the film crew somehow missed capturing Tony's flight on film.

Tony was always innovating, pushing the boundaries. During the annual Port Sydney Regatta one year, he asked me to MC a water-ski show. Tony pulled eight beautiful Port Sydney girls out of the water behind the 80 Mercury that day. It took 1000 yards to get them all up but they did it. During the show, Tony did circles on a banana ski. He also skied on a paddle with winter ski boots clamped to winter harnesses.

He formed a human pyramid with Ted McClure and Glen Stayer. Then he formed a larger pyramid of five people including Paul Johnson and Carol Mackenzie. On one occasion, Tony was able to tow twelve girls behind the 80 horsepower Merc but only after a second boat had pulled up six girls separately. The first six girls handed a spare tow bar to each of the second six.

Tony's father, Stuart, got involved with the local regatta every year as the official starter. He had a shotgun with blanks to signal the start of each canoe and rowboat race. He is famous for once putting a live shell in the starting gun by accident; he almost killed somebody!

The Lawson family was used to hard work. As a family, they owned and operated a thriving badminton club in north Toronto located near Mount Pleasant called the Strathgowan Club. You'd think they would want to relax during their summer vacation, but not so. For the Lawson men, relaxing meant building something. The Lawsons built two motorboats and they repaired all the Clyffe House canoes.

One summer, Chris Lawson and I built a tree house using lumber scavenged from the old maple syrup factory near the barn while his father supervised. Tony recalled, "The tree fort was used for many sleepovers, but the most famous was the time when a waitress from Muskoka Lodge stayed there overnight. She had missed the bus from Port Sydney back to Toronto that morning. My mum and dad were in Toronto, and I was alone. I had been left with strict instructions not to have ANY females stay overnight in the Boat House. So, stretching the rules, I came up with a unique compromise, which allowed her to spend the night in the tree fort, with all the comforts of home, such as water, Ritz crackers, a feather

Waterski pyramid with Tony Lawson, Glen Stayer and Ted McClure; teaching Brad Haig and Doug Donovan to ski; Lawson family boating

pillow, and a telephone line between the tree house and the Boat House. I served breakfast to her the following morning, and drove her to the bus that day."

The Lawsons were active members of the Port Sydney Yacht Club, Tony remembered. "The club was started in 1948 using makeshift old, leaking sailboats. Eventually my parents became honorary lifetime members in the 80s." The Lawsons liked to take part in the annual masquerade dance after the regatta. Their costumes were always well done. Today, the PSYC is still a very important part of social life on Mary Lake.

Freda Lawson was a quiet lady. While her boys were building boats, water-skiing, and leaping over docks, she was painting or she would have a group of children at her knee, reading to them with such skill; they were enthralled by the sound of her voice, Tony recalled. "My mother read stories to the children; she also organized square dance parties. She made up little water colour cards with poems for occasions such as birthdays."

The Clyffe House waterfront was never the same after the Lawsons moved to their new cottage across the lake.

THE MACKENZIE FAMILY: NORRIS, MOLLIE, CHRISTINE, HUGH, CAROL, VICTORIA and MICHAEL

The Mackenzie family vacationed at Clyffe House for several years and our families soon became good friends. Both Hugh and Carol were keen to share stories of their holidays at the resort.[15]

Hugh shared the following:

"The Mackenzie Family came to Clyffe House in 1952. It was just after Mum had polio. I remember the day they drove north looking for a resort and came back and told us about Clyffe House. We first went for two or three weeks each summer, staying in the Annex, mostly on the third floor. We did this for several years.

Group photo at the beach in the 1950s
(Mollie Mackenzie front left)

"We rented your parents' home, "Rosemary House", when we started to come to Port Sydney for the whole summer. I still remember the ritual of driving north on July 1st every year, in awful traffic. Although we rented your house in Port Sydney, we still used the Clyffe House beach. Mum went there every day. We also ate at Clyffe House every Sunday. One Sunday, my Dad parked his car outside the dining room and his engine caught fire. He almost burned down the Main Lodge!

"My Dad and Bruce Scott played golf together and also a lot of cribbage; they were great friends. I remember Bruce with great fondness. He had a very dry sense of humour. He was the Village Cop when I was seventeen and I had just received my driver's license. I was driving toward Clyffe House in my father's car, with Mary Power, probably too quickly and likely showing off. Your Dad pulled me over near Waterslynn Lodge. He walked up to the car, leaned in the window and said "So, would you like me to tell your old man?" That was the end of my speeding.

"I remember being in two or three plays at the Dance Hall produced by Mrs. Gundy. I wrote one of them called "The Missing Pills". Debbie Donovan was the Nurse and I was the Doctor. I remember that Arthur Beemer drew a very funny ad for "The Missing Pills" that was posted at the door in the Main Lodge. It was a Proclamation and started with "Hear Ye, Hear Ye" and it was signed by "U. Will Lovatt". There is no question that I got my first love for theatre in the Dance Hall as a young lad and it has remained a lifelong interest and hobby.

[15] Hugh served as Mayor of Huntsville. Recently, he created a local online newspaper called The Doppler. Like many former Clyffe Hosue guests, he has put down deep roots in Muskoka.

"I particularly remember the dances held in the living room of the Main Lodge and Mr. and Mrs. Husband teaching us to dance "The Gay Gordon". I recall your cook, Maude Clarke, baking pies and chasing us out of the kitchen and the smell of turkey cooking on Sundays.

"The Lawsons ran the waterskiing program and it was great fun to be part of it. When I was twelve, Stuart Lawson went to my mother on the beach and asked if he 'could borrow Hughie' for an experiment. Stuart wanted to prove that it was easier for someone to learn how to water ski if they were pulled directly beside the boat instead of behind it on a tow rope. For the experiment, he needed someone who was a good swimmer but had never water skied and that was me.

"In any event, he had this large wooden pole that extended across the boat near the back and out the side. I held on to the pole at the side of the boat and the boat took off. I got up right away but the pole snapped and I was thrown in the water. I kicked one of my legs into the propeller. "Fortunately, Stuart had immediately killed the motor so the damage to my leg was not great but it required eighteen stitches and I can still feel the indentation in my leg today.

"Most, if not all, of the five Mackenzie siblings think of Clyffe House as an important part of our formative years. Many lifelong relationships started there for me and certainly I would not have spent the last forty-five years of my life in Huntsville were it not for Clyffe House."

The Mackenzie family is another example of a multi-generational friendship: my son Andrew was an usher at Hugh's son Matthew's wedding. My sister, Mary and her husband Paul are very close friends with Hugh's sister Carol and her husband Paul Johnson.

I asked Hugh's sister, Carol, to recall her many summers spent at Clyffe House. Carol has the unique perspective of first being a guest and then an employee, as she worked as a waitress for my mother.

Carol wrote the following:

"I never remember not spending a summer as a youngster at Clyffe House. I remember staying in the Annex. It was great fun having Debbie Donovan so close by. I remember losing a tooth and for about three nights the tooth fairy failed to do her duty. I realized later that the parties were too good in the "green room" and my parents kept forgetting.

"We moved to Cay and Bruce Scott's home, 'Rosemary House', because Vicki had arrived and their house in the village better suited our large family. I was devastated at the move and would be up and on my way over to Clyffe House in the morning before anyone else had stirred. I remember the path of long grass that is now Mary Lake Crescent and how I hated walking through there in the early morning as the dew soaked my shoes. I also remember one early morning when I made it to the Dance Hall and there was a huge snake curled up in the middle of the road. So I went back to the Homestead and eventually Vivian Gundy came onto the screened porch, saw me and walked me past my horror.

"Bruce Scott was good fun and a great friend of our father. He, like my dad, was also very musical and that combined with their Saturday golf game, gave them lots of common interests. It was a Sunday ritual that after the Clyffe House turkey dinner at noon, those two would be at the horseshoe pit with other guests and the game would go on forever. I never minded because if nothing else was happening, I always had the big swing that hung from the tree by the gully.

"Doris Jenner was the wee lady that we all loved. She laughed at everything. She adored her nephew Dave, and her niece Mary. She was a flower thief extraordinaire! Because she was responsible for the altar flowers, I don't think she saw helping herself to anyone's garden as a sin. Cay told the story of Dodie making her stop the car in front of the Inn across from Watson's Cottages. It was lilac time and they had a gorgeous tree. Doris jumped out and snipped away as the owner came out yelling at her. Doris grabbed her last branch and jumped into the moving car to make her getaway. I don't think the owner figured out who had denuded her tree, and the lilacs ended up on the altar that week.

"I remember the beautiful garden Doris had on the cottage side of the entrance into Clyffe House. It ran from the stone pillar right up the road to the turn. Those stone pillars seemed so majestic to me. She also had a massive garden outside the pastry kitchen.

"Your mum was always great to me. One fun story occurred when she was teaching in Huntsville. There was a young male teacher moaning about his inability to find a good tennis game. so your mum invited him to Clyffe House. She said he looked slightly horrified that an old lady would think she could give him a game but was too polite to refuse. The day he arrived was also the day they were having problems with red squirrels in the pastry kitchen. Well. the game went on and this man came off the court exhausted. badly defeated and quite deflated when Dorie came out of the kitchen telling your mum that the offending animal was in the tree right outside the kitchen door. Your mum sent her off for her rifle at which point this teacher tried to talk her out of using a gun. convinced she didn't know what she was doing and offered to do it himself. Of course. Aunt Cay wasn't letting him anywhere near her rifle. She took it from Doris. saw the squirrel. and fired. Two squirrels fell out of the tree. dead. His jaw dropped and she never let on that she hadn't seen the second squirrel. gave Doris back the rifle and asked him if he wished to play another game of tennis. I doubt if he ever forgot that day.

Clyffe House waitresses in 1965 (from left: Mary Scott; Debbie Donovan, unknown, Anna Pennick, Carol Mackenzie, unknown, Olena Oleshnia)

"I also remember the spring between the beach and clay mountain where our mothers used to stash their beer to keep it cold. I do miss that spring. but not all the hauling of water that we had to do in order to provide each room with its own jugful!

"It was at a dance at the Clyffe House Dance Hall that Paul and I first got together as a couple. Mary and I used to go down there early and check out all the coloured lights around the room to make sure they were working. We had such fun there and were blessed with a remarkable group of friends – many of whom we still have as friends or acquaintances today.

"From childhood to adulthood. Clyffe House has always figured largely in my life. From being a toddler with Mary to dancing at her wedding. passing through the grounds on our walks even now and seeing those magnificent buildings. I hope it never goes away!"

Carol and Paul Johnson now own their own Mary Lake cottage in the same bay as Clyffe House.

THE OGILVIE FAMILY: DAVID, ELEANOR and SUSAN OGILVIE

David and Eleanor Ogilvie first came to Clyffe House in 1953 with their daughter Susan and their pet dog. Skippy. They also rented the Scott family home in Port Sydney. but they spent most of their time at the resort.

"Clyffe House plays a large part of my fondest memories of younger days. and later with my two older girls. Lynda and Christine." recalled Susan. "Clyffe House was indeed a place where Dad could totally relax. away from his demanding job."

"I remember Dad. who was a natural floater. falling asleep in the middle of the lake. floating on his back. and drifting out to Crown Island. Stuart Lawson finally came to his rescue (at Mom's anxious request). I also recall the many evenings spent in the kitchen of the Main Lodge with the various families. I always felt rather special to be a part of the 'family' of Clyffe House."

Susan summarized her father's career: "Dad was born in Montreal. and left school after grade eight to work and help support his mother and brother. Through hard work and self-education. he became Director of Blue

Cross. Then, along with Premier Frost, Health Minister Paul Martin, and two doctors, he worked to develop OHIP and was General Manager of OHIP. Finally, he became Canadian General Manager of Holland Life Insurance Co. during which time he was able to enjoy many trips across Canada and abroad with his wife."

Susan's father David was very kind and took a special interest in me. When I was about twelve, Mr. Ogilvie said, "Why don't you try steering my car along the road to Clyffe House?" I was game to try until he sped up a little too fast. Sue recalled, "Of course, I still laugh at your driving lesson with Dad (and me) which ended rather abruptly in the deep ditch!"

Years later, Sue and her husband Bill Harman stayed with their children on the second floor of the Annex.

THE PIGOTTS: MARJORIE (1904 - 1990), EDITH and HILDA

The Pigott sisters began coming to Clyffe House in the 1950s. They had immigrated to Canada from Japan in 1940 after experiencing an earthquake and a war. Marjorie fell in love with the natural beauty of Muskoka. She and her two sisters would walk together around the Clyffe House property absorbing the feeling of being close to nature. "When painting a flower, I feel like a flower," she said. "When painting a meadow, I sense the mood of it." In those days, one of her favorite walks was through the field between Clyffe House and the waterfall.

Marjorie was an artist and had trained in Japan for twelve years at the Nanga Art School. Her talent was absolutely extraordinary. She would put on demonstrations in the Clyffe House dining room painting small five by seven pictures. Cottagers from around the area would watch in awe as she quickly and deftly created flower petals with a single stroke, having loaded her camel-hair paintbrush with two or three colours at once. The result was a flower petal with perfect gradations of shade and colour. She used the "wet into wet" technique whereby the paper was saturated with water and the watercolours were applied quickly while the paper was still damp. She would display twenty or thirty of her paintings around the large dining room perimeter and they were always eagerly purchased by the guests. Marjorie donated the money from the sale of her smaller demonstration paintings to Christ Church, Port Sydney.

Marjorie Piggott painted cards to raise money for Christ Church

Her sister Edith was her manager, but also her toughest critic.
The quality of paintings released was so high that her work hangs in every major gallery and club in Canada and also in major corporate headquarters such as IBM, Sony and Imperial Oil.

Unlike the Group of Seven who captured the beauty of dissonance, that raw beauty of granite rock and wind-swept pine, Marjorie focused on the quiet inner beauty of the flower petal and the deep hush of the pine forest. There is a spiritual quality in her paintings, as if she could see the hand of God in every living natural plant and flower. Muskoka transformed her traditional Japanese art and her art transfixed her viewers.

THE SZAKALLOS FAMILY: IRENE, LOUIS, SHEILA and MARGARET, 1960-1973

The story of the Szakallos family at Clyffe House is remarkable. Louis and Irene defected from their Olympic track team and found refuge in Canada after the Hungarian revolution of 1956. Just as my great-grandparents, James and Fanny, had come to Canada with very few possessions, so too did Louis and Irene, arriving with very little 77 years later.

On April 11, 1993, Irene wrote the following letter to my mother:

"Dear Cay,

"It is a pleasure to recall the wonderful years we enjoyed being patrons of Clyffe House and knowing you and Dorie.

"In 1960, while searching for a place to holiday, we noticed the sign "Welcome to Clyffe House". We parked and took the path to the lake and felt a very special feeling of joy when we saw Mary Lake. It was breathtaking!

"We spoke very little English since we had just arrived from Hungary in 1957. The first night, you Aunt Cay along with Aunt Dorie and the other guests made us feel so welcome. There were many questions and you listened with much patience as we told you of our story of escape from Budapest. Louis and I had gotten married a month before and had no means of a honeymoon. So for us to find you was indeed a stroke of luck. You and Aunt Doris ran a hotel nobody could visit just once! So, as did many others, we returned year after year.

"Clyffe House was to us a magical place: great food, hospitality, charm, warmth and ageless, interesting, wonderful people from every walk of life. As my daughters, Sheila and Margaret, were growing up, their lives were enriched by our visits. They enjoyed the wonderful meals, picked wild flowers and berries, played in the lake and made many friends along the way. I can never thank you enough for all the special events you, Aunt Dorie and the gang created just for us, like the birthday for Margaret (the candy trees made by Aunt Doris, and the bicycle built by Doug, Louis and the kids).

"I feel privileged to have been touched by your friendship and to have many of the happiest times of my life tied to the history of Clyffe House. Thank you!"

Contributed by Irene Szakallos (April 1993)

THE CONRAD FAMILY: FREMONT, MILDRED, MARCIA and GLENN

Throughout the past century, we have welcomed many American guests to Clyffe House. Marcia (Conrad) Wood continues to vacation with us and was happy to contribute her memories to this book.

"My father, Fremont Conrad, was a copywriter for an advertising agency in Milwaukee. He also inherited a flock of prize-winning Rouen ducks from his father, John. Fremont's "hobby" farm included a flock of almost a thousand ducks. He maintained his downtown day job, but was a farmer nights and weekends.

"When it was time to go to the Canadian National Exhibition every August, my dad chose about one hundred of the best birds for competition. While the ducks stayed at the Ex, we drove up to Clyffe House. I can remember going swimming, fishing, playing tennis and hiking with my family. David Scott would lead the hikes and challenge any and all to a tennis match. Doris would place fresh flowers from her garden on all the dining room tables. Cay would arrange the nightly entertainment, including Canadian travel movies. Bruce Scott would take my dad to the ideal fishing spots on Mary Lake.

"My dad brought up some ducks to Clyffe House once and your mother built a pen for them behind the White Cottage. I remember Fremont surprising the waitresses by presenting them with a duck egg and asking if the cook would prepare it for his breakfast.

"When I was ten years old, tragedy struck. My brother, Glenn, drowned at a summer camp on his fifteenth birthday. We still stuck to our routine of coming to Port Sydney, but it must have been difficult for my parents. Afraid that "lightning would strike twice," my parents never allowed me to swim far out from the dock or slide down the falls at the Dam.

"As a young teen, I remember attending the weekend dances at the Dance Hall and walking into Port Sydney over the dam with Peter Donovan and his friends. In the mid-to-late 1960s, we would hang out in the Annex and listen to vinyl records of Gordon Lightfoot, the Byrds, the Beatles and the Rolling Stones. I remember we played silly, juvenile practical jokes on the waitresses and housemaids, but they always forgave us.

"My parents encouraged me to bring my best essays and original stories from school, so I could participate in the evening talent shows in the Main Lodge living room. I would read a poem or essay to the gathering. I remember a tall, slender, white-haired lady, Fleur Marsden, who played the piano. She once told me, "Marcia, keep your head out of the clouds and your feet on the ground, and you will go far." I brought my guitar with me in later years to play and sing for the Clyffe House residents and guests. We had a hootenanny in the dining room, and I sang folk songs by Peter, Paul and Mary, Bob Dylan and Gordon Lightfoot.

"In 1974, Fremont drove the ducks to Toronto by himself and got them all into their cages at the CNE. Then he went back to his hotel room and drew his last breath.

Marcia concluded, "Today, I live in Denver, Colorado. I am a copywriter in the marketing department of a life insurance company. I've kept my head out of the clouds and my feet on the ground. I know a good thing when I see it, which is why I returned to Clyffe House in 2007 with my husband Mark, after an absence of more than 35 years. I hope to return and bring my grandchildren with me."

Contributed by Marcia (Conrad) Wood (September 2007)

THE LUCAS FAMILY:
WALTER, MILDRED, JUDY and MIKE, MATTHEW and ERIN

The Lucas family had been coming to Clyffe House for decades; Judy and I found her grandparents' names in the resort register in 1937. Judy writes:

"I was thrilled when I was asked to write about my memories of my family holidays at Clyffe House. Those memories now include my children, Matthew Rowntree and Erin Nella and, in the summer of 2007, my grand-daughter, Francesca. She is the fifth generation of the Lucas family to vacation at Clyffe House.

"My family first came to Clyffe House in 1937, seventy years ago! As the guest register confirms, both my maternal and paternal grandparents, Mr. and Mrs. William Woan and Mr. and Mrs. J.W. Lucas, respectively, first vacationed at Clyffe House in the summer of 1937, accompanied by their children, Walter Lucas and Mildred Woan. In September, 1938, Mildred and Walter were married and honeymooned in the Boat House.

"Clyffe House was a summer community that included guests who stayed the entire summer. We were fortunate to spend two wonderful weeks enjoying the fresh air, filled with the fragrance of pine trees and warm earth, sandy beach, clear brown Muskoka water, friendships and hearty meals.

"As a child, I remember approaching Port Sydney and reading the sign "Home of 500 nice people and one old grouch", and we knew who he was! Then we could see Mary Lake from the top of that hilly road. I remember the wave of excitement as my father drove through the stone gates of Clyffe House. My brother Mike and I would quickly head for the lake to see what had changed and who was there.

"The days were filled with loosely structured activities. A school bell would ring to announce each meal. Drinking water was obtained for meals from the spring located below the front lawn, at the foot of stone steps. That was where Dad cooled his beer.

"After breakfast, our family would walk to the falls at Port Sydney. We would cross the dam and visit the general store in Port Sydney. After lunch, it was an expectation that everyone would have a rest from 2 pm to 3 pm. A sign, hand-written by Cay on the Annex verandah, asked people to be careful not to slam the screen door. After 3 pm, we were free to go to the lake for a swim.

"Our parents would get together on the second floor verandah of the Annex often with other guests and frequently with Cay, for a libation before dinner. As children, it was hard to resist climbing the iron fire escape ladder between floors in the Annex.

"I realize how fortunate we were to roam and explore the land and the many granite outcroppings. My brother remembers feeling that, as a young boy, he was the only person in the world who knew of those special woodland places.

"My memories of the dining room include the long table reserved for the large Donovan family. I remember the Lawson men who dressed in their white flannels and jackets, reminders of an earlier time. I remember the floral arrangements that Doris put together and placed on white tablecloths. Meals were one of the highlights of the day, home-made, nourishing, and always with seconds.

"In the summer of 1962, Cay hired me as a waitress. That summer I canoed with fellow waitress, Shirley, all the way to Huntsville on our day off, returning at sunset.

"In September, 2007, I returned to Clyffe House and stayed in the same Boat House where my parents had honeymooned, sixty-nine years earlier. Clyffe House has given me warm and pleasurable life-long memories and taught me about the magical lure of nature. Each time I return, I am reconnecting with a very important part of my past."

Contributed by Judy Lucas (February 2008)

Clyffe House waitresses in the mid-1960s
(Judy Lucas on the left)

CHAPTER FIVE: THE STAFF AT CLYFFE HOUSE

Throughout its many decades of operation, Clyffe House has had a great number of loyal and memorable employees and contractors. During the American Plan years, the kitchen was staffed with two cooks and four or five waitresses. In addition, the resort also employed a handy man and a handy boy. The handymen handled day-to-day repairs and general maintenance and their duties were based on their areas of expertise. The more challenging jobs such as carpentry, plumbing and electricity were handled by specialists. Fortunately, we were able to hire local people such as Alex and Harvey Hughes and later, Tom Spivak, Bert Booth, George Stephenson, Gary Henderson, Jim Steel and Daryl Vipond to tackle the more difficult jobs and help solve emergency problems. Today, Rob Orr, John Orr, Bill Quan and Dave Pringle repair and update the resort each year. Howie Crockford and Ross Orr cut back the encroaching forest and provide cords of firewood for the five fireplaces and three fire pits.

Once the kitchen closed, Clyffe House employees consisted of a handyman and two or three cleaning ladies. Our head housekeeper, Gloria Stickland, began working for my mother in 1978, and continued to work for Clyffe House every year until she retired in 2013. She worked every Saturday in July and August, only missing four Saturdays over her 35 year tenure. Gloria helped my mother year-round and took care of her house in Port Sydney until she died. My mother was especially fond of Gloria, was very grateful for her loyalty and thought of her as a good friend.

This chapter contains the memories of some former Clyffe House employees.

THE HUGHES FAMILY: ALEC, DAISY, GORD, DOUG, HARVEY and JIM

Born in 1900, Alec Hughes was a carpenter, plumber and handyman who worked at Clyffe House for 40 years. His sons, Doug and Gord, worked alongside him.

I interviewed Doug in 2006.

"I started working at Clyffe House when I was fifteen, in 1950," Doug told me. "I cut the grass and helped my Dad with the plumbing and carpentry. I worked all summer and it took me that long to earn enough to buy my first rifle. It was a .22 and cost me $17.00."

Doug's mother, Daisy, was a nurse. She sometimes helped nurse Clyffe House guests, including Sidney (Muirhead) Haig one summer.

Doug remembered cutting ice with his Dad for the refrigerators at Clyffe House. They cut it in the bay above the dam. Jim Hughes brought his team of horses and a long sleigh to transport the ice blocks through the snow-covered meadow to Clyffe House. It was a long gentle slope from the river to Clyffe House, which made transporting the heavy ice blocks much easier than cutting in front of the lodge because of the hill there. They would drop off some blocks to fill the ice house behind Fanny Jenner's Homestead. Then they would fill the big ice-house behind the Main Lodge by sliding the blocks up a long plank. They filled between and around each row of blocks with sawdust. As late as 1947, Clyffe House still used ice for refrigeration. There was a large walk-in concrete refrigerator in the middle of the icehouse.

After Robert Jenner's death, Doug and his father were "on call" at Clyffe House. If the large piston water pump broke down, they would leave whatever other jobs they might be on in Port Sydney and rush to the aid of Agnes Jenner and her daughters, Cay and Doris.

Doug recalled that the worst job was cleaning the septic beds. In those days, individual clay tiles were used in septic beds and they became clogged after a number of years. The solution was to dig up the bed by hand and clean the tiles. A piece of asphalt shingle was placed over the one-inch space left between each tile. Today, all the septic tanks at Clyffe House are much larger, modern systems that must be approved by the Ministry of the Environment.

Doug's uncle Harvey looked after the electricity at Clyffe House. He replaced the early "knob and spool" wiring with metal-encased wiring. Before 1960, the control panels for the whole resort were inside a small shed at the rear of the Main Lodge. The shed is still there today and although it is now used to store equipment, we still refer to it as the Power House.

Jim Hughes provided "horse power" for Clyffe House for over thirty years. In addition to transporting the ice blocks, Jim returned in the spring to launch the raft. Robert and Agnes also rented his cows to provide fresh milk in the 1920's and 1930's. Jim provided fresh meat for the Clyffe House dining room until after World War II.

My family will always be grateful for the loyal support and hard work of the Hughes family.

CLIFTON TRAIN

I first interviewed Clifton Train on March 2, 2007. He was 80 years old.

"Your mother and your aunt Doris were wonderful with me," Clif recalled, with a slight catch in his voice. "My mother had died when I was only eight years old. When I turned sixteen, my father decided I should work in the summer. One of the Cowley Fathers from Bracebridge recommended that I apply at Clyffe House."

"Your grandmother Agnes was a very hard-working woman. The cook had quit that summer and she had to take over the cooking duties. My job was to cut up the lamb into chops and roasts for the Thursday dinner. My butcher block was a huge slice of oak tree standing on three legs."

Clif continued: "Agnes and Doris would order fresh lake trout every week. It was brought across from Whiarton by train and stored in the walk-in refrigerator. On a really hot day, if I had been working hard, I would go up and lie on the ice to cool off. It was my job to take ice to the guests from there.

"I remember that your dad, Bruce, was kind. I used to walk to Port Sydney to get the mail. 'Take my motor boat for the mail,' your dad said. I went past Rocky Island which had recently been purchased for $1,400. Your dad asked me, 'Why don't you buy that?' I wish I could have.

"Your dad was very happy, as we all were, to learn of the Japanese surrender in 1945. He celebrated by shooting the red ball off the top of the flagpole with a 12-gauge shotgun.

"When I was working in the shed, I noticed acetylene powder lying around. Your grandfather, Robert, used to manufacture acetelyn gas in a little shed in the gully by the spring. I advised Doris to get rid of the powder because it was dangerous.

"I was the handyman at the resort for three summers. I used to sleep in the little bedroom at the top of the staff stairs on the left. The waitresses' bedroom was across the hall.

"Doris was a hard worker like her mother, but very shy. The place wouldn't have run without Dorie in the background. Your mother, Cay, was a beautiful woman. She looked after the front end, the public side of the business. She organized dances in her Dance Hall.

"Your mother also organized literary readings in the Main Lodge living room. She had lots of talent to draw upon. Poet Wilson Macdonald, editor and author, Robertson Davies from Peterborough, radio host Walter Bowles from CBC all vacationed there with their families during the war. Wilson Macdonald was especially entertaining. He was a long-haired poet. He drove up in an old car with his wife and child. Your mother would arrange for him to recite.

"Other creative guests included Johnny Burt who arranged music for the CBC. He stayed upstairs in the Dance Hall for three weeks and sent his arrangements to CBC by mail. Raymond Massey's son, or maybe it was a nephew, stayed for a couple of weeks. He played the piano.

"I was always worried about the huge water tank on the hill on the west side of the valley. It was built like a huge vertical wine barrel, oak staves held together by iron rings that could be tightened. By 1945 it was leaking badly. The big piston pump down in the pump house had to work and work to keep that tank filled up."

As I thanked Clif for his interview, it was evident that his Clyffe House memories were still a source of joy to him; I could hear it in his voice.

ROY "BERT" BOOTH

When Andy Beemer retired and moved to Muskoka, he bought a house in Aspdin. There he made friends with a number of people and was eventually elected President of the Du Ya Wanna Snowmobile Club. It was through the club where he met Bert Booth who agreed to become the handyman at Clyffe House. For roughly thirty years, Bert did carpentry and repairs at the resort. When I began converting the resort to housekeeping, almost every building needed to have a kitchen added, walls moved, stairs built, dry wall installed, and plumbing either ripped out or new bathrooms installed. Each January, I would outline the work in general in a letter to Bert, and he would line up the plumbers and electricians. Each spring, I arrived at the resort to find that the work had been completed and always to a high standard.

Bert was also responsible for turning the water on and off each year, which involved draining the pipes so they wouldn't freeze and break over the winter. The housekeeping resort had eighteen toilets, 38 sinks, seven dishwashers, ten showers and tubs to dry and over 2,000 feet of pipe to drain, but I never worried about it when Bert was on the job. Since his retirement, I have taken over his difficult job of winterizing the water system, and I appreciate Bert now more than ever.

COOKS AND WAITRESSES IN THE FIFTIES AND SIXTIES

Clyffe House has always prided itself on a high level of repeat business. During the American Plan years, it was especially important to have excellent waitresses since they had direct contact with the guests at least three times a day. The pay wasn't very high, but the tips made up for it. Many of the waitresses came from the city and so the opportunity to spend time in Muskoka was part of the compensation for the hard work with little time off.

The Clyffe House waitresses were responsible for setting the tables and serving three meals. Between breakfast and lunch, they cleaned the hotel rooms. They had two hours off each afternoon between three and five, and the evening work usually ended around eight o'clock, leaving them with plenty of time to party.

Since most of the waitresses were from out of town, they lived in the staff quarters, which were located above the kitchen and woodshed. You can imagine the trouble that a group of young waitresses could get into living away from home in a shared accommodation each summer.

The cooks were usually local women and were seldom young. There was also a "kitchen woman" whose job was preparing the vegetables for the cooks and doing the dishes. After 1950, a commercial Hobart dishwashing machine was installed, which made dishwashing much more efficient.

MAUDE CLARKE

Maude Clarke was the cook at Clyffe House in the 1960s and early seventies. In 2007, I interviewed Ellen Swan, who worked with Maude as a waitress in 1971, and asked her about Maude. "She was a strong personality," recalled Ellen, "she was in charge of the kitchen and she was full of life and down to earth."

For many years, Clyffe House employed one cook to prepare the main course and a second to bake desert, but Maude did both jobs and she was excellent. The waitresses often would sneak down from the staff quarters late at night to steal an extra blueberry pie out of the refrigerator.

Maude's daughter Donna recalled that Doris and Maude had only one conflict: "Doris wanted to slice the pies into eight pieces and my mom wanted to cut only six slices." Cay played peacemaker. "What difference does it make?" she asked. "You give the guests as many pieces as they want anyway!"

ELLEN SWAN

Working at Clyffe House was Ellen's first job at age sixteen. "I had just come from Germany," she told me. "I didn't speak English very well yet. I remember telling a guest that dessert was 'strawberry cake short'. Maude said, 'Don't worry about it. The guests are a kind-hearted, understanding lot'. I wouldn't be where I am today without her," Ellen said, "she was like a second mother to me."

Cay was Ellen's English-as-a-second-language teacher at Huntsville High School. "I invited your mom to my sixteenth birthday party in January 1971," recalled Ellen. "Then she offered me a job at Clyffe House."

Ellen remembered one unique Clyffe House ritual, the "send-off tradition". When guests would leave, especially guests who had come for many years, everyone, including all the staff, would gather on the terrace to wave goodbye. "Clyffe House was the only lodge I worked at where they had such a send-off," Ellen stated.

VESTA HAMPSON

Vesta was our cook for several years, and she and Maude worked together at one point. Her pastries, especially her butter tarts, were loved by guests and staff alike.

DORIS (BOSWORTH) MCKENZIE

Cay Beemer's 80th birthday party
(from left: Doris McKenzie,
Cay Beemer and Nancy Fielding)

Doris was a Clyffe House waitress in the 1960's. She writes:

"I started work at Clyffe House when I was sixteen. I was a server, kitchen helper and housekeeper. I did not want to wait on tables and Cay said that was fine. I could work in the kitchen and do housekeeping. Little did I know she had other plans! On my first day, I was the only one working when the Haig/Donovan family had arrived. She put me straight to work as a server. I just needed that little push. I loved the job and gained the confidence to do it.

"I waited on the Haig/Donovan family during my years at Clyffe House. Their table ranged from six to sixteen people – a great family! Doug Donovan was full of fun, always playing tricks. Peter was a picky eater and he always wanted a peanut butter sandwich. Helen Donovan was a lovely lady. She once took the three waitresses, Helen (Clarke) Pearson, Nancy (Flynn) Fielding and me, to Toronto for an end-of-summer shopping trip.

"The Rices were another memorable family and were lots of fun. Mr. Rice always went for an early morning walk and was waiting for breakfast when we came downstairs. He said we were too slow. One day he showed us "how to do it". He put on an apron, stood in the doorway of the kitchen, called out to everyone as to what they wanted for breakfast and then called the order into the kitchen. That was a much faster way, but he only lasted for a short time.

"Making beds was also part of our job. We were always in a hurry to get that done so that we could have a break before lunch. If it was a day when we were especially tired, we might sneak in a rest in one of the beds in the Annex.

"Maude, Hazel and Vesta Hampson were the cooks and they were really good. We used to break a corner off of the butter tarts and say, "Oh, we can't serve these to the guests." They were always unflappable and made our job very easy.

"Doris Jenner was a very kind person. We would tell her we were hungry at night and then hear her coming up the steps to our bedroom with a big tray of tea and goodies for us.

"Cay Scott was always more serious. Of course someone had to be! There were a lot of us who were not. To get us to clean our room when it got really bad, she would tell us the health inspector was coming and he was going to check our room. She was always very fair though and always gave us time off if we needed it and included us in any resort activity.

"Her husband, Bruce Scott was our musician. He always played the organ while we cleaned up the dining room after the evening meal. He had a great sense of humor and would play any tune we requested. Our favorite was "As Time Goes By".

"Stuart McDonald was the grounds keeper. He would eat with us at the staff table, and would get so upset with us for coming to the table with curlers in our hair and for colouring it. He did enjoy talking with us and we got along well.

"Our afternoons would consist of swimming and water skiing at the beach with the guests. In the evenings, we would walk through the bush to the 'bright lights' of Port Sydney, and maybe help ourselves to a cold beer out of the spring on the way.

"We were famous for our pranks. Our favorite was bending silverware on the table of another waitress when she was not looking. We only did that to people we knew had a good sense of humor. Also a pail of water dumped on the good night kiss of a fellow worker below our bedroom was always fun. Water fights were fun too, unless Dave caught you. Late night raids on the walk-in refrigerator also sometimes occurred. The next morning we enjoyed watching the cooks ponder as to what they thought they had left there the day before.

"I remember that the last year I worked, minimum wage came in. We had to be paid $1 an hour and have days off. That seemed to change things. We had to keep track of our hours and Cay was more watchful that she was getting value for her money. Before that we got around $60 a month plus tips and paid $20 for our room and board.

"My years at Clyffe House were great. We seldom had a day off, but we had every afternoon free if we had all our work done. We didn't mind though, as we were having fun. There was always something going on. It could be a ball game against Pine Lodge, movie night in the living room, or my favorite event - the talent show. There were always the Canada Day celebrations under the big tree by the dining room. Cay would always lead us in the singing of 'O Canada'."

Contributed by Doris (Bosworth) McKenzie (2007)

Over the years, several stories involving the waitresses have surfaced, but I have a feeling the best ones are still being kept a secret. Years later, not long after I was first married, I noticed that some waitresses had listed their boyfriends in black marker on the roughly-boarded bedroom wall of the staff quarters. I took photos of those lists before I renovated the staff quarters, turning it into a rental cottage.

Doris and her fellow waitresses, Helen and Nancy, remained in Muskoka and currently live in Utterson, Port Sydney and Huntsville, respectively. Interestingly, my younger daughter Carolyn met Doris' younger daughter Aimee at V.K. Greer elementary school in 1990 and became friends without knowing about Doris' connection to Clyffe House. They are still very close friends, and Aimee was Carolyn's Maid of Honour when she got married in 2011. Carolyn and Andrew also went to school and became friends with Helen and Nancy's children – again, without knowing about the connection to Clyffe House.

CHAPTER SIX: THE FOURTH GENERATION

DAVID & ARLENE, 1975 - present

I often find myself reminiscing about the people and events at Clyffe House over the years. Born in Bracebridge Memorial Hospital in 1943, I grew up in two very different worlds. I spent the winters living in my family's home, across the street from Watson's General Store in the quiet village of Port Sydney. My days were filled with school, badminton games at the Community Hall, piano lessons, and in the winter, skating on Mary Lake. But when summer rolled around, that's when the real adventure began.

Each spring, my parents moved my sister Mary and me across the lake to Clyffe House, which at the time, was run by my mother and my aunt Doris. Clyffe House has always catered to families with children, and my earliest memories consisted of summers spent running around with friends with a variety of activities at our fingertips: tennis, croquet, archery, badminton, horseshoes, swimming, fishing, canoeing and rowing, to name a few. The later years found us waterskiing, competing in regattas, enjoying bonfires and attending Saturday night dances at the Community Hall.

But it wasn't always fun and games in the summer: I also learned the value of hard work. I started working at Clyffe House at a young age doing odd jobs around the hotel, such as bringing firewood to the various fireplaces, carrying water from the spring to the dining room and to bedrooms as guests checked in, painting and gardening. My mother also had me organize movie nights, dances, tennis tournaments and marshmallow roasts. As a teenager, I worked in the kitchen washing dishes and I remember feeling proud that I could keep ahead of five waitresses using the old 1950s Hobart machine. Being the only male worker in the kitchen also had its advantages.

Cay Scott with her children David and Mary in front of the Main Lodge

The local people my mother hired also taught me a great deal: handyman Stuart Macdonald taught me about carpentry; Alec Hughes explained the plumbing system and how to change the leathers in a piston pump; and the head chef taught me how to cut New Zealand spring lamb into chops and roasts. I admired the tough handymen, some of whom had farms of their own, who could mow the large Clyffe House lawns with a push mower. I never had to split a lot of firewood, but I remember Jim Thackham, a nearby farmer from Beaver Meadow Road, who, at the age of 60 could split several cords of wood at a stretch. As my mother used to say, "When you hire a handyman who also owns his own farm, he works for you just like he works at home: hard and steady."

Sure, some of my jobs were boring (weeding the garden) and some were dirty (digging up septic systems), but others I absolutely enjoyed. One of my responsibilities as a teen was to set up a movie theater in the Main Lodge living room every Sunday night to show National Film Board movies. These were superb movies that the NFB circulated to the various resorts every summer. When I was sixteen and had my driver's license, I would drive down to Divine Lake Lodge (now Trillium Resort) to pick up the movies each week. It was a miracle that I didn't kill myself speeding on the washboard gravel road (at 25 miles per hour, you don't feel the washboard). I was exposed to many award-winning films, which the guests all loved, and so did I. The favourite was "Morning on the Lievre (River)" which followed two men in a canoe down this beautiful river in North West Quebec, providing stunning autumn images to illustrate Archibald Lampman's poem of the same name. Spontaneous applause usually followed any showing of this masterpiece.

Operating under the American Plan, coupled with the tendency at the time to take longer summer vacations – most guests came for two, three, four or even nine weeks in those days – meant that my family got to know our guests quite well. So that explains, at least in part, why so many of the guests had such a strong influence on me. Long-time guest, Freda Lawson, who often held the children at the resort spellbound by reading stories, helped to create my love of language. It was further fostered by the many poetry readings of guests Ed Barrington and Arthur Beemer. I was introduced to photography by several Clyffe House guests, a hobby I pursued for many years. I remember Ron Maitland, in particular, demonstrating the impact of detail in macro-photography. Painting was another talent that several guests brought up with them from the city. I remember Marjorie Piggott demonstrating her "wet into wet" Japanese style of painting, and Arthur Beemer, member of the Toronto Arts and Letters Club, explaining the principles of artistic composition in his landscapes as I helped him hang a selection of his watercolours in the dining room every August. I am reminded of the talent of both of these latter artists on a daily basis as I have several of their pieces hanging in my home.

Music was another important part of the Clyffe House experience. Many guests would bring their instruments up for the summer; for example, I have vivid memories of Stuart Lawson playing the violin. My parents were both talented piano and organ players. Throughout the year, my mother would drive me many miles to various piano teachers and my father taught me his special style of playing the piano modeled after the famous Charlie Kuntz. Both guests and staff have commented on the memory of my father entertaining the guests by playing the piano in the Main Lodge living room after the evening meal.

Aside from the arts, there were many other things to learn, and again, many of the Clyffe House guests had a hand in teaching me. I learned how to play tennis: Andy Beemer taught me his tennis serve; Doug Haig helped me with my grip and stance; and Don Ivey taught me humility. Tony Lawson taught me to water-ski. His father, Stuart, asked me to help him repair canoes. David Ogilvie first showed me how to drive a car.

I left home at age nineteen to attend Trinity College at the University of Toronto to study English and history. After university, I stayed in the city to work and raise my family, but continued the tradition of moving my family to Clyffe House each summer. We always stayed in the Annex, and each of my four children shared the same experiences I did as a child: playing with a wide variety of young resort guests; swimming; fishing; building tree houses; roasting marshmallows at bonfires on the beach; taking swimming lessons in Mary Lake which was often quite cold in those early morning hours; and walking to the general store for candy and ice cream.

As one can imagine, I have accumulated a lot of stories from all my years at Clyffe house. Many of them have already been shared elsewhere in this book by other guests, and there are others that I simply cannot tell. One that comes to mind (without naming any names of course) involves a young waitress who spirited her boyfriend up to the third floor of the Annex one night. Guests were apparently awakened at two in the morning upon hearing the wild cry of "GERONIMO!" Apparently, that cry was repeated by some of the younger guests in the dining room the next morning. I think the waitress quit that same day.

There is also the story of the young chore boy who teased the waitresses to the point where two of the older (and apparently stronger) waitresses grabbed the boy, sprayed him with a garden hose and locked him in the walk-in refrigerator. Thank goodness the Labour Relations Board was not active at that time. The young man quit the same day.

While we never had any lawsuits, we unfortunately did have one guest die: a gentleman was fishing with his son near Crown Island and died of a heart attack. Apparently, he had a large pike on the line. That was the only death, but there were some close calls. Tony Lawson could have died when he water-skied into the main dock while filming a water-ski show for CFTO television. I also had a ten year old boy fall out of a tree and land on a rock one night during a marshmallow roast. When his parents arrived on the scene, having been summoned by a panic-stricken older brother, his mom said, "Oh, this is a regular occurrence with my son." She was amazed that he had been at the resort already seven days without hurting himself.

Years later, one of my guests arrived on a Saturday afternoon, had a few drinks, ran down to the lake, jumped off the dock and broke his leg. Soon after, I put up a sign on the dock warning, "Shallow Water – NO DIVING". That guest still rents a cottage from us now, some 25 years later.

On the topic of signs, as all our guests know, there has never been a shortage of signs at Clyffe House. Especially when my mother ran the hotel, there were handwritten signs posted everywhere. While they were quite plentiful, I did not object to any of my mother's signs. One of them gave notice of "Quiet Hour: 2 pm – 3 pm". The idea was that the guests might want to have an afternoon nap. The real reason, I later learned, was that my mother wanted to have an afternoon nap. I always admired my mother's beautiful handwriting. Her graceful letter formation would undoubtedly remove any sting that her sign content might convey. In his youth, her father had travelled by train all the way to Whiarton to take penmanship lessons; he clearly imparted the care and skill involved to his daughter. This skill was not passed on to me.

My mother and Doris ran the resort quite successfully for many years, but by the beginning of the 1970s, Clyffe House was in economic trouble. A few families such as the Haigs, Donovans, Lawsons, Lovatts and the Hoods were still coming back each summer, but many of the guests had purchased their own cottages in Muskoka, or by now were spending the summers travelling to Europe or other international locations. Clyffe House was also unable to charge enough money to cover the escalating costs of providing food and upgrading the accommodation. At the time, a resort with small bedrooms in frame buildings with communal bathrooms at the end of the hall might still have been viable in some parts of Europe, but in Ontario, it was becoming obsolete.

I soon realized that serving meals was a lost cause at Clyffe House, and I decided to close down the kitchen and began planning the conversion to a housekeeping operation.

CONVERTING TO A HOUSEKEEPING RESORT

My mother and Doris had already converted the Boat House, the Upper Dance Hall and the White Cottage into housekeeping cottages. At the rate of one conversion per year, the necessary changes were made to convert the Main Lodge and the Annex. The Main Lodge was converted into four separate cottages. The front portion of the building became a five-bedroom, two-story apartment with a forty-foot living room, which retained the name the Main Lodge. The former dining room was converted into a separate unit with five bedrooms upstairs and a very large living room with large dining area and eat-in kitchen downstairs and was aptly named the Dining Room.

The old kitchen area became a four-bedroom, two-story apartment called the Jenner. In the new kitchen in the Jenner, the original staff dining table was left in place (and is still there today). During the conversion, the huge wood cook stove was removed and a brick fireplace discovered behind it. Finally, the old ice house surrounding the walk-in refrigerator was renovated and turned into a storage area and the old staff quarters above converted into a two-bedroom apartment appropriately called the Ice Palace.

The three-story Annex was renovated into a four-bedroom cottage on the ground floor. It retained the original 50-foot verandah across the front and the unique stone fireplace made of hundreds of small, beautiful Muskoka stones. The second and third floors of the Annex were no longer rented. However, they were used by my family until we built our new house on a hill adjacent to the resort. Currently, the two upper floors are being used for storage.

By 1988, the conversion was almost complete and it was the end of an era. For almost ninety years, a major component of the resort's success, and a huge part of the summer tradition, was serving excellent, home-cooked meals. Ironically, it was the cost of serving food that had almost sounded the death knell of the business.

Once complete, the housekeeping resort consisted of thirty-one bedrooms in nine cottages capable of sleeping 65 people. The closing of the second and third floors of the Annex meant the loss of sixteen bedrooms so the maximum capacity of the resort dropped significantly as compared to the old American Plan days.

Clyffe House as a housekeeping cottage resort in 2016

For many years, Arlene and I spent our summers on the second and third floors of the Annex. Helen Donovan rented the main floor of the building for the entire summer. Due to the layout, we passed by Helen's living room door every day as we entered and walked upstairs. One night, as I was returning from having a septic tank pumped, Helen was entertaining her family at dinner. The devil seized hold of me and I invited the truck owner and his wife in for a drink. Somehow, we ended up in Helen's living room and the septic truck driver began telling stories. He, at one point, told Helen's family that "their poop was his bread and butter." Weeks later, seeking revenge, Helen's kids invaded my living room upstairs with a conga line. They danced right through our cottage and back down the stairs. Helen's family has become our extended family.

In the summer of 1989, with my wife Arlene and my younger son and daughter in tow, I moved home to Port Sydney. Eventually, we built a house up on the hill beside the Clyffe House valley. My younger children attended V.K. Greer Elementary School and then Huntsville High School, just as I had done, and were often told stories of their grandmother, Cay Scott, by their teachers, who had once been her students. I myself continued to teach, also at Huntsville High School, and even took over hosting the year end staff party at Clyffe House, the way my mother had done for many years before me.

When you grow up in a resort environment such as Clyffe House, you absorb the lifestyle and it becomes a way of life. My mother and Doris were not interested in building the material capital of a resort; they were much more interested in developing relationships with their guests. I would hear questions such as, "What colour do you think we should paint Mrs. Haig's bedroom?", or, "Should we buy a new bed for Mr. Beemer?", or after Arthur Beemer came for 80 plus years to the same room, they started asking, "How can we get Arthur to stop using the jerry pot and start using the washroom down the hall?"

Summer traditions are a big part of life at Clyffe House. I have often observed guests getting up at dawn each day to enjoy the tranquility with an early morning swim, canoe or walk. Others show up on the first day with their annual "to do" list anxious not to forget any of the activities they've been reminiscing about since the previous summer. I fondly remember one former guest, Ron Knowles from Ottawa, who would literally hug the giant white pine near the Main Lodge each year when he arrived.

My children have all told me how fortunate they feel to have spent their summers at Clyffe House. As kids, they worked hard and played hard the same way that the four generations of Jenners did before them: they cut grass, chopped wood, painted buildings, bailed boats, and raked the beaches. They also slid down the Port Sydney waterfall, participated in the Regatta, organized games and tournaments and made many friends. They all love to canoe, camp and water ski and my sons are both avid fishermen.

The Port Sydney Regatta is still one of the highlights of the summer for my family. In the early 20th century, it was held in front of Clyffe House. In my lifetime, it has always been held on the Port Sydney beach. My grandfather used to help organize events; my mother and her sisters and brother used to take part in the races; and now, my children and grandchildren enjoy participating. I have photographs of both Greg and Andrew as teenagers sitting at the table with all their ribbons and medals spread out in front of them. They have a great rivalry with the Stayer and Woodcroft families in the annual canoe races – especially the War Canoe and the LeMans, where large trophies are on the line.

My son Greg fondly remembers our annual canoe trips down the Muskoka River, skeet-shooting in the Fall down Sunset Trail, scaring his sister Cathy and her girlfriends while they were camping by pretending to be a bear (I couldn't chastise him, as he reminded me I'd done the same thing to him). Greg described "the feeling of anticipation and excitement that I felt as a child each time we turned off the highway and onto South Mary Lake Road at the beginning of the summer".

My daughter Cathy also wrote about her summers at Clyffe House. "I appreciated the beauty of the land from a very young age. Aunt Doris (Aunt Dodo as we called her) taught me about gardening; she showed me all the spots where the strawberries and blackberries grew. I remember stuffing our pant cuffs into our socks while we gardened together in the spring to protect our ankles from the bugs. My brother, Greg, and I loved the water and would swim endlessly. Those early days were pure bliss."

My younger daughter, Carolyn, decided that she and her fiancé, Gregor Bush, would marry at Christ Church and asked to hold their reception at Clyffe House. Up until that point, I had always refused to host weddings at Clyffe House, but in her case, I gave in, as I could see that it meant a great deal to her. We put up a large tent on the tennis court for a dinner and dance, and 150 guests danced the night away. It was a glorious September day, truly a day to remember, and the event was written up in Wedding Bells magazine. Of course, there was a tradition of family weddings at Clyffe House already: my grandmother Agnes; my mother Cay; and my sister Mary.[16] In addition, Mary's children Jenna and Scott married Kyle Sparling and Allison Campbell, respectively, on the Whitehead's dock which is adjacent to the Clyffe House dock, and Scott and Allison hosted many of their guests at Clyffe House for the weekend.

My son Andrew married Melissa Litrenta in 2015 before being transferred overseas to Shanghai with his employer, a large American computer software company. Andrew has been invaluable in our effort to compete in the age of the internet: he designed the Clyffe House website, added social media connections, and developed a sophisticated reservation system. He and Melissa plan on moving back to Port Sydney once they return from Shanghai.

The sixth generation is well on its way: Cathy and Ken Murray have Meaghan and Kiera; Greg and Sandra Scott have Kristian; Carolyn and Gregor Bush have Kaitlyn and Lauren, and Andrew and Melissa welcomed Maya in August 2016 while living in China. All four of my children love the Clyffe House property and its traditions and have always helped to make our guests feel welcome.

---

[16] Cay and Bruce Scott were married at Christ Church on September 14, 1940; Mary and Paul Whitehead on July 8, 1972; and Carolyn and Gregor Bush on September 17, 2011.

The Scott family, 2013 (from left: Carolyn, Gregor & Kaitlyn Bush; Kiera Murray; Andrew Scott; Arlene & Dave Scott; Cathy, Ken & Meaghan Murray; Kristian, Sandra & Greg Scott) photo credit: Kelly Holinshead

I often say to my family how lucky we all are, and I think writing this book has made me realize just how true that is. We are the beneficiaries of the hard work and courage it took for my great-grandparents to travel to, settle on and farm the rocky Muskoka landscape. We are able to enjoy the resort that my grandparents, Robert and Agnes Jenner built over decades of determination and hard work; and that my mother and aunt continued to run each summer for many years. We cannot forget the fortitude of the early resort guests making the treacherous journey from the city, enduring day-long trips by train, ox carts, and steam boat. We are both amazed and thankful.

On numerous occasions, former guests have phoned or dropped in to reconnect – often they haven't been back to Clyffe House in several decades – and while they might look a little older, the sparkle in their eyes as they recount their Clyffe House memories is always the same. One of the things I personally cherish is knowing that my family and I have in some way contributed to the lifelong memories of these loyal Clyffe House guests.

CHAPTER SEVEN: FASCINATING LOYAL GUESTS

1975 - Present

The change to a housekeeping operation meant that many of the American Plan guests no longer wanted to vacation at Clyffe House, primarily because they wanted their meals provided. New families came, and new traditions were created.

It is impossible to acknowledge each of the many families who vacationed at Clyffe House year after year. The four families that contributed to this chapter each returned for more than twenty years. The Murphy family rented the Boat House for over 30 years, beginning in 1975; the Pangman family rented the Dance Hall for twenty years, from 1981; the Morris family first came in 1979, and is still vacationing at Clyffe House each summer – a 37 year tradition; and the Lucas family first stayed at Clyffe House in 1937.

In addition to the contributing families, I would like to mention several others who returned (and in some cases, continue to return) for many, many years.

First, the Uba family: Ed and Lorraine, along with their children Lisa, Andrea, Janice and David, vacationed at Clyffe House beginning in 1982. They stopped coming when the children were in their late teens, but returned when their grandchildren were born in the 1990s. I converted the dining room into a housekeeping apartment specifically for the Ubas who rented it for the entire summer. Ed was an avid fisherman; he would save up the bass that he caught and put on a large fish-fry at the end of his stay, which he shared with us and some of the other lucky guests. Like so many of our Clyffe House guests, the Ubas eventually bought their own cottage in Muskoka.

Reynolds, Sargent & Thompson families - 20th year at Clyffe House in 2014

Next, the Sargent family. Bob and Jacqueline came to Clyffe House beginning in 1982, usually for a month, for almost twenty years. Jacqueline's parents often stayed with them; their boys, Jared and Sean, grew well into their teens here. Jacquie, with her infectious laugh and leadership skills would often organize various activities and events, including tennis tournaments, and costume parties. One summer, I even offered Jacquie the job of Recreation Director.

Lori and Paul Sargent (Bob Sargent's brother) have been coming to Clyffe House with their friends Jennifer and Mike Reynolds, and Joy and Doug Thompson for twenty-one summers. They have a complete photographic record of their children growing up summer after summer at Clyffe House. To commemorate their 15th year anniversary, they had a group photo printed on T-shirts. In 2014, which was their twentieth year, I joined them for a drink one evening and was lucky enough to witness a very touching toast "to our Clyffe House family tradition" delivered by Lori and Paul's son, Brett.

The Browns: Gord Brown and his wife, Marie, from Ridgetown, Ontario, began vacationing in the Main Lodge in 1990 and returned each summer for over twenty years. Both have recently passed away and we miss them dearly. Marie was an avid swimmer who swam twenty laps along the buoy line every day, and I always looked forward to my annual conversations with Gord, while enjoying the view from the front verandah of the Main Lodge. Their daughter Carol Brown continues to vacation here with her family.

JEAN AND JOHN MURPHY

Jean and John Murphy first discovered Clyffe House in 1975. They were visiting their daughter, Anne, at nearby Pioneer Camp. They met Carol and Paul Johnson at the Port Sydney Yacht Club who told them about Clyffe House. In 1976, they rented the Boat House for the first time, and were still vacationing at Clyffe House 35 years later until John died in 2011.

"Our daughter, Anne, married Dr. Bob Turliuk of Burlington. They usually spend two weeks in the Boat House every year. They love to windsurf and play tennis. Soon their two children, Stephen and Jennifer, became Muskoka enthusiasts. The whole family loves the water, especially sailing and windsurfing. One summer, they helped to organize the "Clyffe House Olympics" with the Sargents, Judy Woods, the Keluskys, the Rocas and the Droughans.

"I tend to cower inside during thunder storms while my husband loves to sit on the verandah in a metal deck chair and watch the lightning!

"John and I love to listen for the loons at night. We love to see the beaver and mink. The deer come down to drink in the early morning. John helps the Ministry of Natural Resources by doing an annual loon count on Mary Lake.

"For thirty-five years, we have enjoyed the sunsets from the Boat House verandah, walking through the forest or over the dam to Port Sydney. We go each year to the autumn turkey dinner at the Community Hall and watch the fireworks."

Contributed by Jean Murphy (2007)

THE PANGMAN FAMILY: JOHN, CONNIE, ALEX AND JENNIFER

"In the late seventies, John and I had two wonderful small children, one with special health needs, and so, when it came to finding a place "at the lake" for them, it had to be special too.

"Dave, you personally invited John to your house in Oakville to see slides of Clyffe House. The rest is history, over thirty years at Clyffe House!

"We rented the bottom floor of the old blue Dance Hall with the shuffle court still visible on the floor and the kitchen where the bandstand used to be. It was Doris's home in winter and she rented it out in the summer.

"Doris was a good friend to the artist. Marjorie Piggott who had. over the years. given Doris enough wonderful paintings to turn the Dance Hall into an art gallery! There were no locks on the doors and it used to worry us city folk that some of those paintings might go missing! But of course it never happened.

"We had breakfast most mornings in front of a roaring fire. sitting in Doris' rocking chair. Sometimes we would finish our daughter Alex's treatments early to get down to the beach before the mist had lifted off the water. It was quiet then and wonderful to canoe and to enjoy the local wildlife. including the loons. the otters. and the beaver. It was a meditation spot for me. Alex has overcome cystic fibrosis to become a successful recording artist accompanied for several years by the late Jeff Healey on piano.

"I remember sitting in the lake on deck chairs because it was too hot to sit anywhere else. When we would arrive. there was always a telephone call to welcome us. There was no TV. and that was a good thing!

"I remember puzzles. games. crafts. family tennis games. and walks to the waterfall. We loved to canoe and were even brave enough to paddle up Mud Creek one year.

"I remember the boat ride when you drove us around Mary Lake. Dave. and told us about the history of Muskoka Lodge. Dead Man's Island. Grunwald Resort. and Camp Glenokawa.

"I remember being treated almost like family. and it was very good. The weeks at Mary Lake were a chance to recharge our relationships with each other and with the world.

"Thank you so much. Clyffe House!"

Contributed by Connie Pangman (January 2007)

Connie's daughter Jennifer is a ballerina and Alex Pangman (as Connie mentioned) is a jazz singer. Alex recently received a doubler lung transplant. She released her latest music video. "Undecided" in 2014.

THE MORRIS/CHURCHILL FAMILY

Morris & Churchill families - Clyffe House guests for over 35 years

Just as the Mackenzie family had done during the 1950s, Bev and her family first rented my mother's house in Port Sydney, "Rosemary House", and spent most of their time on the Clyffe House beach. In her second summer, Bev moved to the Dance Hall.

"I have a treasure chest. It is not filled with expensive jewellery, family heirlooms or souvenirs from travels to exotic places. Rather, tucked neatly and safely inside are memories, none more precious than those from family vacations at Clyffe House.

"It all began in 1979 with an ad in the Toronto Star which led us to Mary Lake and a family tradition which would forever more define summer. For the past thirty-one years there would be no summer without the anticipation of the first look at the Dance Hall as we drove along the winding road past the White Cottage, around the Main Lodge finally reaching the two storey building painted the perfect blue with its own piece of Muskoka architecture right outside the door – the "rock".

"My son Justin was fourteen months old that first summer, too young to climb the rock but it would serve as a challenge to master from then on. Several years later his new baby sister Simone spent her first summer at "our cottage". For the next fifteen years we measured their growth with a photograph atop the rock.

"The days were full with leisure. For one month we ignored timetables and swam, canoed, fished, made sand castles and forts, caught butterflies, constructed toad houses and hunted for salamanders, snakes and cicadas, and walked to the General Store in Port Sydney for ice cream.

"We loved the simplicity of the three small bedrooms off the main living area, enjoying the sweetness of the children sleeping so close as we read or watched old movies on our small TV.

"For the past ten years, the Churchills have joined the Morris' to make the family vacation complete. My sister Jan (her husband Doug and son Hayden) and my brother Paul (his sons Evan and Neil) have spent two weeks together in August at Clyffe House. Our time together as a family has been the truest of precious memories. Family dinners, campfires, sing-alongs, games and long talks into the night could not be bought at the most expensive hotel.

"The highlight of the vacation is our annual "Dance Party" where young and old compete for no prize or trophy, but to be declared winner of the talent competition. Tina Turner, Celine Dion, the Village People vie for the title. Our good friends from Georgetown (the Sargents, Thompsons and Reynolds) have even resorted to dressing grown men in tight leotards to steal the show. The ladies have been known to sneak down to the dock late at night with fudge and ice wine for fortification to test the water "au naturel"!

"My treasure box is overflowing with memories of children growing up, the feel of the silken water of Mary Lake, sitting on the dock alone with my thoughts or my best friend, staring at the dark, majestic pine trees on Rocky, walking up the hill from the lake in the dark, exclaiming each time as though it were new, at the spectacular vision of the blue building in the trees with its glowing windows, morning coffee on the dock when the lake is like a dark piece of glass and evening cocktails as the sun sets and the children fish for the same unlucky bass. The generations are proving that the memories will continue as we have welcomed Simone and Mike's beautiful children Olivia and Sam to the Dance Hall. We are truly blessed."

Contributed by Bev (Churchill) Morris (2010)

This year, 2016, was the 37th year for the Morris/Churchill family at Clyffe House.

JUDY WOOD & LARRY ONISTO

Judy Wood and her children Kathleen, Bruce and Matthew rented the Dining Room for many years with Judy's cousin Ron Knowles and his family. Judy was a vibrant, friendly and athletic woman who loved Mary Lake. In fact she enjoyed it so much that she and her husband Larry Onisto eventually bought a property on Mary Lake Crescent. Judy's children now return in the summer with their own children. and continue to enjoy all the activities and summer traditions that they experienced when they were kids.

I often enjoyed a game of tennis with Judy and Ron and considered them dear friends. I was highly honoured when Larry asked me to give a eulogy upon Judy's untimely death. It is fitting indeed that Judy's ashes are interred in the Christ Church columbarium overlooking Rocky Island and Mary Lake which she loved so much.

THE HAPPY BOOKERS

The Happy Bookers are a Collingwood book club that has been vacationing at Clyffe House since 2006. Each year they choose an author and bring the books to life with menus. music. and costumes. which recreate the mood and culture of the selected works. Some of the themes have included: Jane Austen: the Roaring Twenties. Great Gatsby: The Western. and Lonesome Dove by Larry McMurtry.

The Happy Bookers Club from Collingwood celebrate the 60s

We are very fortunate to have wonderful guests who return year after year. While I can't list everyone (my apologies to those I have missed). I wanted to be sure to include some of the families and groups who have been long-time guests. who haven't already been mentioned above.

- Ginny Thiessen. Bill Simmons and their children Nicole. Bryan and Ben
- The Koning family
- Anthony and Ann Shuttleworth and their children Angus. Larry and Susan
- Robert (Beau) and Norma Thompson and their sons David and Paul
- The Downey family: Kae and Joe Downey and Mike and Mado Downey and their extended family
- Isabell Koebel. Geoff Steel and their son Anthony
- Ken and Ene Lomp and their family
- Mark and Cheryl Romanko
- Patsy and Kevin Crandles and family
- Julie and Phil Anderton along with their triathlon club
- Gord and Marie Brown and their children
- Li Feng and Min Zhang along with their family and friends
- Rheal and Beverly Benard and their children Ben and Ray
- Steve and Emi Baxter and their extended family

AFTERWORD: THANKS FOR THE MEMORIES

Which is the oldest resort in Muskoka still run by the same family? I'm proud to say that the answer to this Muskoka Trivia question is Clyffe House. Having been in operation for 130 years and through five generations of the Jenner family, Clyffe House has literally withstood the test of time. How do I explain the success of Clyffe House? It is the result of a lot of hard work, a lot of sacrifice, a love of the land and, more importantly, the people it attracts.

I am now a member of Resorts of North Muskoka, a group of family-owned and operated resorts, several of which are third and fourth-generation operations. One of my fellow resort owners, Brian Tapley from Bondi Village Resort, established in 1905, told me he loves the lifestyle that is an integral part of this business. Rob Wallace of Foxwood Resort coined an inspiring phrase, referring to his love of Lake of Bays, saying, "My soul breathes here." We have that in common. We love Muskoka; we love meeting new people; and we derive satisfaction when guests return year after year. Unfortunately, the old resorts have been disappearing over the past 60 years.

Hopefully, the remaining core group will survive and continue to offer a traditional Muskoka experience through which families can introduce their children and grandchildren to the inspiring beauty of nature. The old resorts offer an authentic Muskoka experience which the newer, larger, condo-style resorts cannot. While many factors both in and out of their control may prevent it from happening, I hope my children can carry on the Clyffe House tradition. And while I realize that it may not happen, I can't imagine Mary Lake without Clyffe House.

Many people have asked me when I'm planning on retiring, but to be honest, I love what I do. Granted it tires me out more now than it used to, but I still can't imagine a summer without busy Saturdays welcoming new guests and saying our annual goodbyes to those heading home. It's in my blood and it's made me who I am today. Had I asked my mother, or her father, Robert, or his mother, Fanny Jenner, the same question, I think they would have had the same response. There seems to be a genuine sense of hospitality handed down from generation to generation, which I believe was originally rooted in my family's Christian upbringing. Together, these characteristics seemed to create a chemistry to draw the guests back year after year, decade after decade, and in some cases, generation after generation.

I want to offer a sincere thank you to the many guests who have been so loyal to Clyffe House. You have all been patient with our shortcomings, supportive with your suggestions for improvement and appreciative of my family's efforts over the decades to ensure that your vacation with us was always a memorable one.

ACKNOWLEDGEMENTS

I have many people to thank for their contributions to this book – unfortunately, a few of them are no longer with us.

To all my contributors, thank you for taking the time to record your memories.

Thank you to everyone who proof-read the manuscript and offered valuable suggestions, including: my sister-in-law, Wilma Irwin and her good friend, Willa Murray; my son Andrew; my friend and former teaching associate, Tom Clark, of Huntsville; author and editor, Bob Attfield of Huntsville (I thoroughly enjoyed his book "Browning Island, Lake Muskoka", Fox Meadow Creations, 2000); and my good friend and neighbour, Ryan Kidd.

The editor of the final version of this book, my daughter Carolyn, is an excellent writer (well-trained by the Huntsville High School English Department). She offered crucial suggestions regarding the structure and style of the final manuscript. Only when the book passed her thorough examination did I dare to publish it.

Thank you to all the Clyffe House guests and employees, past and present, for without you, none of this would be possible.

Thank you to my wife Arlene for wearing various hats over the years in order to help run Clyffe House: gardener, book-keeper, and back-up housekeeper, to name just a few; and especially for her patience throughout the process of writing this book.

And finally, thank you to all my children and grandchildren who bring me great pride and joy each and every day.

APPENDICES

INTRODUCTION

There were many members of the Jenner family who were not directly involved in the development and operation of the resort. Their unique stories are summarized in these appendices.

APPENDIX A: THE CHILDREN WHO WENT WEST

James and Fanny Jenner had seven children between 1870 and 1883. The children were, in order: Frederick, Alfred, Robert, Ida, Roland, Alice, and Charles. Of the seven children, only two remained in Port Sydney: Robert and Ida. The remaining five moved to western Canada and the United States. Five led long and successful lives; unfortunately, Alfred and Charles both died in their late twenties.

FREDERICK JAMES JENNER, March 22, 1870 - 1965

James and Fanny's oldest child, Fred, lived a life worthy of its own book.

I first met Fred at Clyffe House in the summer of 1964. At age 93, he had driven 3,600 hundred miles with his daughter Evalene from Seattle via Dawson Creek. He was retracing the interesting path his life had taken him.

As a teenager, he worked on the farm at Clyffe House and in the shingle mill at Port Sydney. In 1890, at the age of twenty, Fred moved to Vancouver where he worked in boat building and shingle milling.

He then moved to Edmonton, Alberta in 1896 where he operated a gold dredge and a river trading boat for about two years. In 1899, he traveled down the Athabasca and the Mackenzie River and crossed The Divide and into the Yukon River Valley. He then prospected in Alaska for about four years. He did not become rich and instead became an amateur dentist, as he was the only person in Anchorage with dentist's forceps. Using liquor as a sedative, Fred pulled a lot of teeth. The miners were glad to give him a poke of gold dust to ease their pain.

Fred then moved to the state of Washington, where he married Frances Jean Jennings of Marysville on July 5, 1903. He first worked in shingle milling around Arlington, and later, with his youngest brother Charles, he went into the lumber business in Stillaguamish Valley. In 1916 he turned to dairy farming and raised purebred Guernsey cattle near Oso, Washington. Finally, he turned to raising beef cattle until he retired in 1962 when he moved to his daughter Evalene Wasson's home in Seattle, Washington.

I dined with Fred and Evalene during the time they spent at Clyffe House in 1964, and I remember him saying he wished he had patented his idea of having two helicopter rotor wings going in opposite direction so as to combat the counter-spin problem. He was quite the Renaissance man. His daughter Evalene became an engineer at a time when women seldom did. While in Port Sydney, Fred and Evalene attended the 90th anniversary service at Christ Church where he had been christened in 1870.

Fred and Evalene drove directly home via Sault Ste. Marie, a route 1,000 miles shorter than the 3,600 mile route they used driving east. Evalene was driving a Lincoln, which was quite a contrast to Fred's trip west by train and north by home-made boat in 1899.

ALFRED ERNEST JENNER, 1872-1900

Alfred traveled west to join his older brother, Fred, on the Athabasca River where Fred operated a trading boat. On August 12, 1899, Alfred and Fred set off with two other men, Abel Weeks and Ab Schaefer, to travel down the Athabasca, "just to see the north country".

They started the trip with a large boat with 3.5 tons of provisions, and they lived primarily on fresh game and fish.

They were towed across Great Slave Lake by a Hudson's Bay steamer. The Indians warned them not to go on the lake if the willow trees were even quivering because the winds and storms would come up quickly and swamp them. Even being towed, they barely survived the crossing. They proceeded north down the Mackenzie River to Fort Simpson. There were Hudson's Bay posts about every 125 miles.

When they passed Fort Liard, they traded 200 pounds of martin fur for two bladders of tallow because their diet lacked fat. When they passed through 'the Ramparts' on the Mackenzie River, a narrow stretch with cliffs 150 feet high, Fred calculated that "with a dam in this canyon, you would have over 40 million horsepower at a normal flow."

At a Hudson's Bay post, they learned of the gold rush, and so they decided to cross the mountains into Alaska by going up the Laird River. Since that river was small and swift, they whipsawed spruce lumber and built another smaller boat.

In a letter to his sister, Ida, written on February 16, 1899, after he had returned home to South Edmonton, Alfred passed along news from Fred about Alaska: "Nearly the whole country is covered in up to two feet of moss and when the snow melts in the spring, the moss prevents the country from drying up and the sun causes the stead or fog to rise. As the ground is frozen, nobody knows how deep the miners have to thaw all their dirt with fire which makes a lot of extra work."

Alfred never made it to Alaska. In the spring of 1900, he took sick with Typhoid fever. Alfred died at age 28. He had never married.

IDA SARAH (JENNER) CASSELMAN, March 29, 1875 - February 24, 1931

This brief sketch of Ida's life was provided by her granddaughter, Rhonda Collis.

"I imagine Ida was a good student because, when she was 17 to 18 years old, she went to Normal School (now called teachers college). She taught in Ilfracombe for a while. She married Captain Lyle Casselman in 1904 when she was 29 years old and they had three children.

"Captain Casselman was 36 years old when he married Ida Jenner. He ran the steamer "Gem" through a chain of lakes including Mary Lake, Fairy Lake, Peninsula Lake and Lake Vernon. He also owned a farm on Peninsula Lake.

He died on December, 1918 at the age of 50. He was killed by a falling tree while working in the woods. Ida had to sell the Peninsula Lake farm out of financial necessity.

"My mother, Donna Casselman, was a waitress at Clyffe House in her teens."

ROLAND JENNER, 1880

Roland bought in as a partner in Clyffe House with his mother in 1903. Together, Roland and Robert, the Jenner Brothers, expanded the Main Lodge significantly and built the three-story Annex.

Roland and his wife sold their share to Robert in 1908. Five years was enough for Roland to figure out that the resort business in Muskoka was hard work with too many challenges to make a lot of money.

At that point, Roland left Port Sydney. He first went north to work in the mines, and eventually, like so many others, he settled in the west. He lived in Saskatoon, Saskatchewan and later, in Flin Flon, Manitoba.

ALICE MARY JENNER, January 3, 1881 - July 11, 1966

Alice Marie became a teacher, then a nurse, and eventually a missionary. She moved west and lived in Edmonton until her death. She married late in life.

CHARLES JENNER, 1884 - 1912

Charles was the last to be born to James and Fanny and he was the first to die at age 28. Charles worked with his older brother Fred in the lumbering business near Seattle, and was killed by a falling tree.

APPENDIX B: THE THIRD GENERATION

Robert and Agnes Jenner had four children: Wesley, Miza, Catherine and Doris. All four children were involved in the operation of the resort when they were young. As adults, Wesley and Miza decided to leave Muskoka, although they continued to maintain a close connection to their family and to Port Sydney.

ROBERT WESLEY JENNER, July 12, 1909 - 1985

This biography was written by Wesley's son, David.

"Robert Wesley Jenner always went by the nickname "Wes". He was born in the White Cottage at Clyffe House on July 12, 1909. I remember Dad proudly pointing out the "little red school house" village school down by the river (now called Robin Hood Apartments), which he attended. He mentioned once that all eight grades were in one room with one teacher.

"He was sent off to board with an aunt in Mitchell, Ontario, for high school. After high school graduation, he enrolled at the University of Toronto and graduated in 1929 with a BSc degree in Chemical Engineering. He was a member of Phi Beta Kappa scholastic honors society/fraternity.

"During his time at both high school and university, he spent his summers working at Clyffe House and guiding canoe trips in Algonquin Park and Tamagami. I know that Andy Beemer went on several of these canoe trips.

"When he graduated from the University of Toronto, he could not find a job right away so he wrote to different universities in Canada and the United States seeking Graduate Fellowships. The only reply he received was from Case School of Applied Science in Cleveland, Ohio. He graduated with a Masters Degree in Chemical Engineering in 1932.

"After receiving his Masters Degree, he was hired by Dow Chemical Company in Midland, Michigan, as a research chemist. Dad was sent up to Marquette to inspect the premises and its potential for Dow. He expected to stay in Marquette for two months and ended up staying for the rest of his life. I think that the area reminded him so much of his beloved Muskoka that he never wanted to leave. He was eventually promoted to President of this Dow subsidiary.

"Dad met and courted Mom at Clyffe House because her family vacationed there in the early 1930's. They were married on July 25, 1936 in Toronto. Dad was already working in Marquette at this time and they moved there as soon as they were married. Mom was strictly a big-city girl, but their honeymoon was a canoe trip in Algonquin Park!

"I have some pictures of the last surviving Clyffe House cedar canoe: Clyffe House #2. Will Ruch had it restored and it never leaked a drop. Aunt Mike (Miza Jean-Marie) says they used to race it in the Regatta on Mary Lake by putting on sideboards and a lateen sail. It really belongs in a museum.

"As well, I have Grandpa Robert Jenner's old Model 1886 Winchester deer rifle, caliber 45-70, which a Dr. MacLaughlin from Cleveland, Ohio, gave him. He hunted deer out of Clyffe House. It was manufactured in 1903 according to the serial number."

Contributed by David Jenner (December, 2006)

Wesley and his wife Ethel had three children: Robert, David and Ellen. They became a diesel electric submarine chief engineer, a Catholic priest, and a nurse, respectively.

I met my uncle Wesley many times and will remember him for his intelligence and his love of Muskoka. He always tried to help my mother and Doris solve their business problems and was especially supportive of his youngest sister, Doris.

When Agnes Jenner died in 1952, Wes inherited approximately 300 acres of land in Port Sydney. He and his mother had already sold the Hawkes Road subdivision on Mary Lake. He eventually sold the land where Bridgedale, Mary Lake Crescent and Raymond's bluff are currently located.

MIZA MACDONALD (JENNER) JEAN-MARIE
March 8, 1911 - September 24, 1998

Miza had two sons, Jenner and Ron. The following was contributed by Miza's younger son, Ron Jean-Marie.

"My mother, Miza Jenner, was born on March 8, 1911, in the front bedroom of the White Cottage at Clyffe House. She was named after her maternal grandmother, Miza (Smith) Macdonald, who was related to Sir John A. Macdonald. Miza completed her high school education in Mitchell, Ontario, where she boarded with her aunt. After attending Havergal Girls' School, she graduated from teachers college in 1929 and began teaching in a one-room schoolhouse in Juddhaven, near Minett, Muskoka.

"Mother met my father, Howard Jean-Marie, at her Juddhaven school, S.S. #9. Dad volunteered to start the fire every morning for her. The schoolhouse was located on the Jean-Marie homestead.

Her father, Robert, would drive from Port Sydney to Juddhaven with the horse and cutter to bring Miza home for Christmas. He drove along logging trails. He crossed Three Mile Lake and then across Lake Rosseau from Windermere. Sometimes, my Dad hired James Hughes to pick up my mother with his horse and cutter.

"Mother's second teaching post was in 1931 in Wood Township S.S. #3. The school was a one-room, log cabin. During the depression, she worked at Ryde Township, S.S. #3 Lewisham. Today, that schoolhouse is a hunt camp. Miza boarded with a family who had eight children. They lived off the land, mostly by eating deer and grouse and whatever they could scrounge. Mother told me that every Saturday, she walked sixteen miles round trip, to get the mail at Barkway, and it was a very rough trail.

"On December 24, 1934, my mother married Howard and moved to Juddhaven. She could no longer work because it was against the law for married women to teach school! Mom moved to Toronto and returned to teaching in the late 50s. She taught mentally challenged children for over twenty years.

Like her mother and grandmother, Miza was active in the church. She attended St Hilda's Anglican Church. Mother never got involved in running Clyffe House; however, she must have inherited the hospitality gene because she often entertained friends at her cottage "Windrush" on Lake Rosseau where Father had created beautiful rock gardens, walkways and a goldfish pond. Her favourite activity was paddling her 1917 Lakefield cedar strip canoe on Lake Rosseau which is now part of the Clyffe House "fleet".

"Mother and father are buried in the Christ Church cemetery in Port Sydney near her grandmother, her mother and father, and her sisters, Cay and Doris."

Contributed by Ron Jean-Marie

BIBLIOGRAPHY

Guide Book & Atlas, Muskoka and Parry Sound Districts (Erin: Boston Mills Press, 1879).

Barbaranne Boyer, Muskoka's Grand Hotels (Erin: Boston Mills Press, 1987).

George W. Boyer, Early Days in Muskoka (Bracebridge: Herald-Gazette Press, 1970).

D. G. Creighton, The Commercial Empire of the St. Lawrence, 1760-1850 (Toronto, New Haven and London: University of Toronto Press, 1937).

Innis, Harold. The Bias of Communication, University of Toronto Press, 1951

Ryan Kidd and David Scott, These Memories I Leave to You – The Story of the Mary Lake Settlers (Victoria: Trafford, 2003).

Research Committee of Muskoka Pioneer Village, Huntsville, Lake of Bays, Pictures from the Past (Erin: Boston Mills Press, 1986).

Douglas McTaggart, Bigwin Inn (Erin: Boston Mills Press, 1992).

Women's Institute of Port Sydney, Pioneer Days in Port Sydney (Port Sydney: Knox United Church, 1927).

The Game of Muskoka (Bracebridge: PO Box 306, Bracebridge, Ontario, P0B 1C0).

Printed in the United States
By Bookmasters